Dear Kathry

M000116494

May you fena
on your path!

The Courageous Heart

Finding Strength in Difficult Times

Compiled by Kyra Schaefer

Rosemary Hurwitz
Ch. 8 p. 81

—2020—

The Courageous Heart: Finding Strength in Difficult Times

Copyright © 2020. All rights reserved. Each author in this book retains the copyright to their individual section. Their submissions are printed herein with their permission. Each author is responsible for their individual opinions expressed through their words. No part of this publication may be reproduced, distributed, or transmitted to any form or by any means, including photocopying, recording, or other electronic mechanical methods, without the prior written permission of the publisher.

As You Wish Publishing, LLC
Connect@asyouwishpublishing.com

ISBN-13: 978-1-951131-08-1

Library of Congress Control Number: 2020917064

Compiled by Kyra Schaefer

Edited by Karen Oschmann

Printed in the United States of America.

Nothing in this book or any affiliations with this book is a substitute for medical or psychological help. If you are needing help please seek it.

Dedication

For Dr. Vicki L. High

Table of Contents

Foreword

Courage is only necessary when we face adversity, and in 2020 we are all suited to speak directly on this topic. The courageous voices you will experience in the following text take you through their deeply personal courageous journeys. I would gladly walk beside each of these authors through any challenge.

In the chapters you are about to read, these authors, coaches, and healing professionals also share their approach to meeting any difficult occasion with courage. Finding strength doesn't necessarily look like having a fight or fighting with others; sometimes, it is choosing your happiness and allowing yourself the opportunity to expand a good experience with a great one.

If you have found in the recent months or years that your courage has been maxed out, this book will help you with simple tools and exercises to help you stay on track. Achieving the life of your dreams does take courage and love. Use what you will learn in the following pages to make a difference in your life and the lives of others.

I believe in you, the authors believe in you! You can move through whatever trouble you are facing right now. Let the authors of this book be a touchstone for you as you connect with your courageous heart.

Chapter

One

Facing Cancer with Courage and Gratitude

By Marion Andrews

Marion Andrews

Marion Andrews, bestselling author, Integrated Energy Therapy Master-Instructor, Reiki Master/Teacher, life aficionado, strives to impart the knowledge and wisdom she has gained through numerous classes, certifications, and volunteer leadership positions. In a three-year fight against stage 4 colon cancer, Marion discovered energy healing as the way to restoring her inner self, as well as helping with healing the physical self. Through the different modalities of energy healing, Marion can help you to safely and gently release limiting energy patterns from your past, empower and balance your life in the present, and embody your full potential as you move into the future.

Marion can offer you:

- Relaxing, therapeutic Reiki or Integrated Energy Therapy, in person or distant energy work
- Meditation classes
- Online Angel Classes
- Schedule a 15-minute free video call by emailing or messaging Marion at:

marion@marionandrews.com
585-495-2435
www.marionandrews.com
www.chrysaliswellnesscenter.com
www.facebook.com/marionandrews

Facing Cancer with Courage and Gratitude

By Marion Andrews

I am going to tell you a little about my life and what I am learning as I crawl, creep, walk, run, and slide through it. Initially, I wrote "what I *have* learned," but as soon as those words appeared on the page. I crossed them out and wrote, "I *am* learning." That is why we are here on this earth, isn't it? To keep learning and growing. Perhaps with help from God, spirit, archangels, angels, and guiding spirits, we shall all learn something more. Some small nugget of truth that when you read it, click, snap! It snaps into place. An a-ha moment!

I was especially drawn to the words, mystery and wonder, and those are two of my favorite emotions. We are surrounded by both daily, but sometimes we don't pay attention. I would like to add another word to these two that may help you. Mindfulness is the word I want to add. Being present, being in *the* present. These are words often used in the communities that are in tune with spirit. I had heard some of these words, even used them. But I didn't understand them and absorb them until a few years ago. I have learned some ways to stay mindful and present.

Four years ago, I began a walk down a road with that dreaded disease, *cancer*—specifically, colon cancer. When it was first discovered, it was already at stage 3B, which meant there was a growth, and active cells had wandered out and were growing in some lymph nodes scattered around my abdomen. Say what?

It moved along in the next four years to spread here and there to be re-classified to stage 4. One of the remarkable things of this journey is not that I had cancer show up over and over again but that I am still here and, I believe, here with a purpose.

When the cancer was discovered, it was a total surprise to me. I was shocked. I am one of eight children, and I am the one who ate whole grains and lots of fiber, drank plenty of water, and didn't smoke. What was going on? And yes, I had regular colonoscopies. My one only two and a half years before had been clear with no polyps and no signs of disease.

After the shock subsided, my thoughts were, what do we do next? Somewhere in the back of my mind hovered the idea of "What do I need to learn from this?" It seemed that I wasn't listening to my spirit; my body needed to do something drastic to get my attention.

As an aside here: Pay attention to the messages your body is sending you. It took six months of persistence, saying, "This doesn't feel right," to get the diagnosis. Granted, it wasn't the one I wanted to hear, but one that I needed to hear. Have the courage to trust your instinct.

The adventure—the amazing journey—began. Checking in with myself, this didn't seem to be the time of the end of my human form, but rather, a unique opportunity to learn some lessons and then perhaps, to be able to teach others and help them heal. I knew that it was going to be difficult and would take more than my strength to get through it.

I began to search out spiritual teachers and guides. I learned that healing isn't physical first. Healing is always emotional and spiritual, *then* physical. The manifestation of the disease shows up in the body, but the recovery is always in our spirit.

Meditation became a part of my life at this time. The oncology department recommended meditation as a relaxing, healing technique. The research began. Meditation courses, tips, videos, books, the list went on and on. It was confusing. I didn't know what to do. I decided to jump in, I sat down and tried it. Sitting quietly, paying attention to my breathing, it was terrific. I added soft music and used guided meditations. That was it! I now cannot imagine a day without my morning meditation. It helps me to be present and aware all day. To be mindful and filled with awe and wonder.

I started my first chemotherapy treatments on August 1, 2014. Chemo was an adventure and challenge to my physical body. Each time I went, the toll was higher, but what a great gift it was to me spiritually and emotionally. Because I have always been the giver, I had a hard time being the receiver. Now I had no choice.

I was showered with love and kindness. Special people stepped up in my life to drive me to the cancer clinic. Others brought food. I received hundreds of cards and well wishes. What an opportunity to serve others by accepting their love and care. Another important lesson to learn, we need to be receivers to allow others to give and experience their personal growth.

Cancer came back two more times, and the journey has been a roller coaster ride of chemo, radiation, scans, and numerous doctor visits.

I was meeting with a spiritual advisor for some coaching and a boost in my determination. She helped me to visualize the cancer and then visualize the Archangel Michael using his sword to cut out the bad stuff, and then the Archangel Raphael coming in with his green, healing light to soothe over the place and heal it. I did these daily for the next three weeks until my next CT scan

When the results came in, the scan was clear, the doctor was amazed. He had no reason for what happened. But I knew. A miracle had happened! I know that miracles are happening every day, and we need to live a life of mindfulness and courage to be looking for them.

At this time as well, someone noticed that I referred to cancer as *my* cancer. It was suggested that I stop owning the cancer. My cancer belonged to me, and we don't give up our possessions so easily. A simple change in my vocabulary, changing the simple word "my" to "the," gave me a different feeling. Think about it. Which is easier to get rid of, *the* book or *my* book?

A reminder: be mindful of words you speak and thoughts that float all around in your head. Thoughts are things that become manifest. Be careful what you speak and think into existence.

I have spent a lifetime searching to understand what my purpose is here on earth. What am I supposed to be doing? Am I walking on my path? Am I fulfilling the contract I made when my spirit came here in this body? I asked all sorts of people to help me understand this. I wanted to fulfill my purpose!

Looking back over my life up to now, I see glimpses of what I now know is my purpose. I got married at a young age, and it eventually came apart. I still don't know what that was all about, but I did learn some things from 20 years of that marriage.

I was blessed to bring three amazing human beings into this world. I loved everything about that process. I loved being pregnant, even though I had terrible morning sickness for four to five months. What a graphic demonstration that something exciting and different was happening in my body, genuinely a mystery and a wonder and a miracle. The toxemia, the weight gain—all fascinating responses to the changes within my womb. How wonderful is that? My puny physical self had a share in creating, nourishing, and protecting another body, a loving home for spirit housed in this fragile bag of bones. What a privilege I was given. Sometimes we miss out on the great things in our life by thinking they are ordinary.

Now, I am sure that my purpose is to teach and to heal. In my humanness, my ego says that I need to find that significant, meaningful work I am here to accomplish. I have learned (finally) that it isn't necessary to be grandiose. I was always looking and asking, "What am I supposed to be doing here?" and "Help me find my purpose," instead of merely getting ego out of the way and allowing spirit to shine forth. A purpose can be as small as touching one life. My path and purpose are filled with many small instances when I have been allowed to influence another's life for the better.

One incident that stood out from that time was when I attended a silent women's retreat. Now, if you have never experienced a weekend like that, let me set the stage. A busload of 45 women of varying ages, sizes, and backgrounds descend on the retreat house. This is a marvelous place; quiet and serene. You sense the presence of spirit immediately upon entering the house. Filled with wonder and excitement, we came in, registered, and attended our first of the guiding talks in the chapel. The first message was, "Ladies, the silence begins now. For the next 48 hours, you may only speak when asking a question or at a talk or if there is a genuine emergency. You may choose to speak privately in your rooms when counseling or seeking counsel. The goal here is to turn within, to listen to that voice of spirit that wants to speak to *your* mind and heart."

I invited a friend to this retreat. She was a younger woman whom I felt guided to accompany me. Late the next night, I heard a discreet tap on my door. I answered and welcomed her into my room. We lay on the single bed, head to foot, and I listened to her. She was troubled; her marriage was in jeopardy.

The major problem was that her husband didn't "get" her—didn't fulfill her. I was guided to ask these questions: "Have you told him what you want him to do to help you? Have you explained what you need? Your husband is not a mind reader. He is trying to please you but working blind, with limited knowledge and experience. You can help by talking, explaining, and making your needs and desires known to him." We ended our short, whispered conversation with a prayer of thanksgiving.

Some weeks later, I received a thank you card from her. She credited our discussion as saving her marriage. Things had improved vastly, and they both were much happier as a couple. I accepted her thanks, but knew that I wasn't the author of that advice. I was merely the mouthpiece used to help her. In that beautiful, spiritual, silent place, I was used as a conduit of the words she needed to hear. What a gift I was given! That 30-minute whispered confidence impacted her life hugely and who knows how many others along her path. Isn't that exciting? I *love* being the instrument to affect another's life.

I have also begun journaling. Journaling is a tool to help you to handle all the big and small things that appear in your life. This shows me one of the big benefits of journaling. Getting those words out of your head and onto paper can get you back into the attitude of gratitude that is necessary to maintain a higher vibration in your body. And to heal.

I have a daily journal that also is my calendar for appointments, among other things. Getting the right book required research and many YouTube videos. It involved buying different formats and all sorts of colorful pens. The result is a book I truly enjoy. I can write everything in there. I can be creative; I can be messy. One thing I love to do is turn to a blank page and write in a freeform, stream of consciousness writing. It is a mystery to me that my spirit guides and angels will talk to me through this type of communication. Words flow on to the paper. It is so exciting and fun. Since I am relatively new to this whole idea, it is extremely unusual for me to be doing this and even more vital, trusting this.

I am grateful for every single day and sincerely look at this time with such wonder and awe. This journal entry from early in my first round of chemotherapy reminds me that even when we are 100 percent healthy and vibrant, all we have is *now*:

> “First off, I am feeling *so* much better. Started to turn the corner yesterday and am flying today. I almost wrote “this week” there but realized what I have is *today*. Each of us only has now. I am working on living for right now! I have always struggled with my weight, and I have lived a lot of my life with the thought and plan that goes something like this…I’ll do that when I am thinner, I’ll be able to do _________ when I am thin, or whatever. Or when I’m rich, or when I’m retired. But what I have is now, the present only. I am living each minute, hour, and day to the fullest!”

In the past six-plus years, I have learned a lot about meditation, keeping a great attitude no matter what the circumstances—especially by associating with spiritual people—and how to use a daily journal to keep me present, to keep me organized and growing. I suggest that if you haven’t used any of these tools, you should look into it.

The God of my understanding can be trusted to send the help, direction, and guidance we need. The angels are messengers waiting to deliver it. All we are required to do is show up and be open to receive it.

Be present. Be here. See everything with wonder and mystery. Face each day with courage and joy. It’s worth it.

Chapter

Two

A Woman's Journey into the
Heart of Money
By Kathryn Eriksen

Kathryn Ericksen

As an empowered wealth expert, mindfulness teacher, best-selling author, and former attorney, Kathryn discovered a simple truth—whenever she listens to the messages from her mind, she always makes different choices than when she listens to the music of her heart. Mind messages lead you down a path of believing in lack, limitation, and fear. Heart music opens up your world, where you are a powerful creator and explorer of all things good.

That's why Kathryn created Empowered Way Coaching. She helps women entrepreneurs who have lost sight of their authentic selves in their money relationship. *The Empowered Money Map: The Sacred Feminine Journey of*

Wealth, Abundance, and Peace is her signature coaching program. As her clients learn their sacred money archetypes, uncover their limiting money beliefs, and create a new money story, they transform themselves and their relationship with abundance, wealth, and prosperity.

Kathryn's passion is to guide women of purpose to their authentic and abundant selves, and as they step into their creative genius, they serve the needs of the world. As she loves to remind us, "When enough women believe they are worthy, loved, and divinely held, the world will be healed."

Empowered Way is the path for you if you have stumbled, fallen, and brushed yourself off while you stood back up. Ready to try again, but using a different mindset that includes spirituality, mindfulness, and manifestation. Learn more at EmpoweredWay.com and schedule a free, 20-minute Discovery Session.

Kathryn is also a published author and speaker, and her meditations are available on InsightTimer.com.

A Woman's Journey into the Heart of Money
By Kathryn Eriksen

"If you're invested in security and certainty, you are on the wrong planet." ~ *Pema Chodron*

Women and men are wired differently. The classic *Men are From Mars, Women are From Venus* by John Gray highlighted many of those differences. Mars and Venus each have their place around the sun, but they exist in different orbits, and each has rules and perspectives that seem foreign to the other.

Live on this planet long enough, and you will experience contrast in the ways that men and women use money. Men are more outward-facing and goal-oriented, judging their success by the results of their actions. Women are more inward-facing, relying on intuition and their access to a higher intelligence to guide their actions.

Or at least that is true for women who have journeyed into the *heart of money*.

Unfortunately, in Western society, a woman's way of creating abundance and wealth has been discouraged, denigrated, and degraded. To succeed in today's world requires women to ignore their natural genius, turn away from their inner world, and rely on the ways of men.

But women are from Venus, not Mars. And the success rules that govern Mars do not translate well to Venusians. In fact, the Mars rules are the exact opposite of how Venusians create with the energy of money.

Have you ever felt caught in an invisible web of rules that you didn't understand, no matter how hard you tried? You did everything just like the guys around you, but they seemed to succeed while you still struggled. If you were like me, you turned your "unsuccessful" results inward, condemning, and judging yourself. That inward-turning of disgust, disappointment, and desperation highlights the fact that women don't naturally create abundance following the rules established by men.

Mars rules are not better or worse than Venus rules, just different.

As women, we stand at a crossroads in our evolution. Do we continue to beat our heads against the wall by believing that Mars rules are the only way to create abundance? Is there another way?

Yes! Please join me on a journey into the heart of money. The path starts with what money is, then moves toward the power center, and ends with the treasure of feminine genius.

You are the gatekeeper for your creation of abundance, wealth, and peace. Allow me to share with you how to create abundant wealth as a woman. Peacefully. Naturally. Synergistically.

The journey begins when you discover your limiting beliefs about money.

What is Money?

Money is a fluid concept, reflecting whatever you think about it. Limited or abundant, hard to come by or trust in the flow, money adapts to your beliefs and words like Saran Wrap™ clings to the shape of a bowl.

Money is the ultimate shape-shifter. It can become a monster, snarling and snapping its long, pointy teeth in a fierce show of power. Or it can morph into a gentle wave, supporting your weight as you allow yourself to be in the flow of its energy.

Are these your ideas about money? Take a minute to write in the margin some thoughts that popped into your head while you were reading these words.

A key question to ask is: "What does money mean to me?"

We think we know what money is for, but we are only interacting with our subjective concept learned from others. It takes a courageous heart to step back and be willing to see differently.

Uncover Your Hidden Money Beliefs

Growing up, I received mixed messages about money. My father (a child of the Depression), worked long and hard hours to support the family. His work supplied us with a comfortable lifestyle, but he never seemed happy or satisfied. As a young child, his energy felt like defeat mixed with stubbornness to me.

From my father, I learned that money was a hard taskmaster, that it was elusive and resistant to anything but hard work. Deprivation and limitation were waiting to step in if you relaxed even for a minute. There was no magic or play, only dedication and persistence.

My mother was raised in an affluent household, and the Depression never touched her. She admired money for the status it could provide, but her shadow was the fear of losing it all. Money was a cloak you wore that others admired, but a thief in the night could steal it in a heartbeat.

From my mother, I learned that money was an elusive guest who could turn on you without warning. Money was never to be trusted because your safety was dependent on a quicksilver substance that was always changing.

As you can see from my brief descriptions of my childhood, there were many conflicting beliefs about money, how to relate to it, and what it meant to me. By going on my journey into the heart of money, I became aware of these embedded beliefs, and I could begin to make different choices.

The first step is to begin uncovering the hidden beliefs that you absorbed in childhood. From the time you were born until about seven years old, you naturally absorbed the money beliefs of those around you as yours. At such a young age, your mind is a sponge, with no ability to judge or decipher which beliefs are true or not. These first beliefs about money are probably still running in your unconscious, impacting your decisions, and directing your actions.

Start a money journal and begin observing your beliefs about money, abundance, and your ability to create wealth. It's a daily practice that will yield an informative harvest.

Here are some entries from my journal of limiting beliefs that I uncovered:

- Men are the rulers of money; women are the caretakers.
- Money is a tool and a way to control others.
- It's challenging to support yourself as a creative woman.

Looking back, I can see how I developed these beliefs from my parents' attitudes and beliefs. It wasn't until I began to excavate them that I realized how much they influenced my financial decisions. Once I became aware of these hidden beliefs, I noticed them frequently. In those situations, my awareness became my opening to making a different choice.

Becoming aware is the first step on your journey into the heart of money. When you identify the limiting beliefs about money that you absorbed from others, you begin to notice them. That moment of awareness creates a space for change. In that split second, you have the opportunity to take a deep breath, step back mentally from the situation, and ask whether you want to continue in this limiting behavior. Your decision is entirely yours, and the consequences flowing from that choice also belong to you.

I call this process of awareness, "minding the gap." Whenever you travel in London, the subways always warn you to mind the gap as you are getting on or off the train. That small space between the platform and the subway car is a potential hazard.

On the journey to the heart of money, the space that you create between your habitual thought, and your behavior is full of possibilities. When you mind the gap, you have taken your power of choice back from living unconsciously and habitually.

As you make different decisions about your finances, be aware that regret, shame, and even anger may surface. These emotions are real and spring from your sense of disempowerment under the Mars system. Feel these emotions, knowing and trusting that they will pass through you. Forgiveness and compassion are the companions who support you through this process.

Your choice to live differently—from awareness and decision—is what brings you to the next stop on the journey, how you relate to your power center.

Men, Women and the Power Paradox

When you look up the word "power" in the dictionary, it is defined as "to do, to act, to accomplish, to make things happen." Masculine energy is woven through that definition, and it serves the inhabitants of Mars well. As men discover their power, they accomplish great things.

The etymology, or origin, of the word "power" reveals an even deeper connection to Martians. The word power shares a root with the word "patriarchy." Wikipedia defines patriarchy as a "social system in which men hold primary power."

We live in a patriarchal society. Is it any wonder that you may have felt like an alien living in a world that is foreign to you?

Women have forgotten how to access their feminine power center. Instead of trying to survive in an environment that is not synchronized with feminine energy, it's time to learn about a new way to relate to money.

Women value connection and relationships—to ourselves, our creator, and each other. When we try to thrive using traditional power, it severs us from our strongest qualities. We become disconnected and unable to remain authentic. Feeling helpless, afraid, and alone, we may give up ever having a strong relationship with money.

The good news is that your past doesn't have to dictate your future. You can begin to have a vibrant relationship with money right now. It doesn't matter what you have thought of money in the past, or the fear you may hold for the future.

Change can only happen in the present moment.

A simple but profound exercise is to write letters to and from money. Sit in a quiet space with your money journal, and start the first letter like this: "Dear Money, I have always wanted to tell you that…." Pretend that money is going to read this letter without judgment or reaction. Describe every resentment, betrayal, or hurt that you have ever experienced. Let it all out. Trust that there is an end to the litany of complaints—there always is.

Take a break, walk away, get centered. When you are calm, pick up your money journal and turn to a new page. Breathe in deeply, knowing that now it's money's turn to share with you. The second letter is from money to you. Start it like this: "Dear (your name), I have always wanted to tell you that...." Write down whatever words or ideas show up. Don't filter, judge, or argue. This time is the sacred moment when you allow the energy of money to tell you what it needs.

Isn't it amazing that money can talk to you? When I first discovered this exercise, my concept of money was extremely linear and goal-oriented. I never realized that money is an energy that grows when it is shared freely and received openly. When I discovered how to connect to the energy of money, it made all the difference.

As you begin your journey to the heart of money, remember that you, as a woman, thrive when you feel a sense of belonging and becoming. When women feel part of the whole, their hearts open wide, and the collective consciousness expands. This sense of belonging and becoming is what holds women together, stronger than if they stand alone.

It's our natural genius. It's where we are the most creative, supportive, and visionary. It's our power center.

When we feel disconnected from the energy of money, we are fundamentally disconnected from ourselves. With no sense of belonging or becoming, we have no connection with abundance, prosperity, or wealth. We try to dance with the energy of money, but we don't hear the music.

The disconnect between a woman's innate genius and her ability to peacefully create abundant wealth is wide as it is deep. What is the bridge between the two?

It's your breath. When women go inward and meditate, their sense of connection to the unseen becomes real. It can't be quantified or measured, but a woman knows when she is secure in her relationship to source.

Many of my clients have never meditated. They were hesitant and doubtful, having heard that meditation is hard or that "it's impossible to stop your mind from thinking." Over time, as they trust the process of going within, they discover a beautiful, vibrant inner world, from which they can access their intuition and guidance.

It's the way we are wired. To stay connected to the flow of life, for a woman, is to be alive.

And that is how we discover the treasure trove of feminine genius—the last stop on the journey to the heart of money.

The Treasure Trove

When you have connected to your higher power, the door opens to remember the genius of feminine energy. You have reached the place where the heart of money lies ready for you to connect, surrender to the flow, and dance.

You have three genius centers that support your ability to peacefully create abundant wealth. As you access these energies, your confidence and trust grow, and you have what you need to step into your higher destiny.

The three feminine genius centers are:

- Awareness of your higher self;
- Intuition and knowing; and,
- Accessing abundance as a feminine creator.

When you begin to live from your genius centers, your sense of worth grows, your ability to discern what is supportive strengthens, and your access to infinite abundance is revealed. You move into your presence, knowing your connection with source is the most valuable relationship you have, and you feel safe stepping into your higher calling.

You become the creative force you were meant to be before you detoured into the land of masculine power. You proudly carry your Venusian card, and you discover other women who have also stepped into their genius.

Your creations create ripples in the world because your expression of source energy is authentic, intentional, and guided. Your inner guidance system is fully functional, and the outside world no longer directs or controls it.

You are your own woman, standing in your power.

You know that you are enough, that you are loved, and that you are love. This *knowing* changes everything about how you relate to money, abundance, and wealth. You are fully supported, and everything works in your favor.

Money is no longer a mysterious, unfathomable thing. Instead, it becomes an ideal tool to create with source energy, as you serve others. Stepping into the flow of abundance, giving and receiving equally and without hesitation, becomes the norm, not the exception.

From your deep knowing of worthiness and love, you create magic that transforms the world. Living from your connection to a higher source, your power is expressed, honored, and seen.

You are abundant, wealthy, and peaceful, the hallmarks of a Venusian woman connected to the heart of money.

Chapter

Three

What If?

By Jami Fuller

Jami Fuller

Jami Fuller is the creator and owner of Visions of Light Soul Healing. This talented and intuitive healer uses all her gifts to help build and promote wellness in others. She is down-to-earth and always about self-love. Her teachings are based around filling *your* cup first so that you can set the best intentions for your life. Focused on the law of attraction and all its components, Jami helps to guide others in realizing their greatness through daily gratitude practices, true self-love, and emotional mastery. She is a mother of two beautiful boys and a strong advocate for self-awareness and self-advocacy in young people. She is filled with love and appreciation when the people she works with push through barriers and truly understand how important and powerful they are. There truly is no greater gift than that of another human stepping out of the shadows of self-doubt and believing that they are worth every greatness life has to offer.

She offers Reiki, angelic golden ray healings, oracle card, and mediumship readings, all with intuitive insight, and teaches and mentors in all of these areas. Jami is a hyper, or physical, empath as well—meaning that she connects with others physical pain and can help translate what the physical body is telling about the person's emotional or mental blocks. Our bodies are magical, and once you learn what they're saying, it's easier to move through the challenges and blocks we put in place.

To connect with Jami, email her at
visionsoflightsoulhealing@gmail.com.

What If?
By Jami Fuller

"Fear /fir/: the bad feeling that you have when you are in danger, when something bad might happen, or when a particular thing frightens you." ~ *(2020, May 05) Oxford Advanced American Dictionary*

What is fear? As defined above, it's a feeling, and although an incredibly powerful one, it is an emotion nonetheless, so completely in our power. The first part of conquering fear is to know exactly what the root of the fear is and why it's controlling us. This is probably the most difficult part, and I'll walk you through it all, but first I want to tell you a story.

This is my story. I am merely another being, not unlike you, I suspect, and though my story isn't one of extreme circumstances, I am one of the most courageous people that I am privileged to know.

Even now, the fear of writing this is huge! I've walked away from it so many times, not wanting to put the words down, as then they become increasingly real in some way. What truly inspires me in my story is how, no matter what, I keep overcoming. My fear doesn't hold me back.

Fear shows up every day and in so many different ways. It can come as a physical threat, an imagined threat, or even a self-imposed belief. All of these have been experienced on many different levels in my 40 years of life. From animal attacks, human attacks, psychological attacks, and, worst of all, those attacks that come from self, I have overcome them all.

Abuse is a hard word to swallow and is something that is far too common in my experience, though I won't go into great detail about it. What gets me is why the reoccurring theme? Why does it happen again and again, and the answer is—simply put—fear! Fear keeps its hold on us as an old protective layer. It keeps us safe from the unknown and keeps us from venturing out and doing dangerous things. It also keeps us from expanding and trying new things. It keeps us in a cycle of suffering rather than freeing ourselves from its hold and allowing us to enjoy our unique individual journeys. Remember, this story is about overcoming the fear, and during this narrative, I want you to keep your focus on overcoming.

The simplest instance of fear for me to explain is probably one of the hardest I had to release. This fear was self-inflicted. It is one I created and substantiated by repeated action and beliefs on my part. It came in the form of anxiety and obsessive-compulsive disorder (OCD). These two were the ones I completely engrossed myself in. Anxiety is the body's natural response to fear stimuli. It comes from a lack of the life-threatening/survival kind of fear in today's society and is created by our minds and perpetuated and often exaggerated by our minds as well. This does not negate its severity, nor does it put any form of blame or fault on the person experiencing it. Anxiety is real, and one of the most successful tools in managing and releasing it, is to externalize it. In essence, the anxiety is an outside factor that tricks the person affected into feelings of fear, thus limiting them and dictating their life in a multitude of challenging ways.

Early on in life, I needed to be the best. I had to have perfect grades, be the most accomplished athlete in multiple sports, be perfect on the outside, have perfect friends, the best boyfriend, and so on, and it turned my inner self into a complete mess. I suffered from generalized anxiety disorder and OCD, as mentioned above, but also had an autoimmune disease, anorexia, and a multitude of other health issues, all stemming from my need for perfection on a strictly superficial platform. I have an over-analytical brain and tended to overthink everything in those early years. I based all of my experience on this goal of perfection and created beliefs that were then reinforced by those experiences. No matter what I did, I was never going to live up to the standards of perfection that I was creating. I blamed my parents for expecting too much of me. I blamed my siblings for being better than I was at things that I had no interest in. I blamed society as a whole for pushing me to feel I needed to be perfect. This was back in the '90s in a time of supermodels. They were physically perfect, so why couldn't I be? My issue was that there was nothing in my mind that was good enough about me, and I feared rejection for not being the best (There it is! The core fear!). I was competing against an imagined portrayal of self that was always changing and never attainable. I tried to kill myself because nobody could love me. I couldn't see how many people actually did love me. I couldn't see how many people looked up to me. I couldn't see the beauty in the imperfections, and the strength it took to step out of the pack and embrace myself. Obviously, I wasn't successful, and I thank my angels every day for their protection and interference, but that's a story for another book.

What this experience taught me was my first step in overcoming fear. If something so grand could fight for me, then there must truly be something wonderful about me. I started to question my beliefs but was not yet equipped to release the fear completely. As I said before, the core fear in my case was rejection—not being good enough. I rebelled. I rebelled against myself, and I rebelled against my ideals. I went to extremes and caused myself more damage than good. I feared nothing, or so I thought and didn't have a strong enough foundation in who I truly was to be able to flourish, and thus reinforced my old beliefs of not being good enough. So, I ran. I was presented with an opportunity, and I jumped in with both feet. It was one of my best choices and brought me to a place of self-discovery. I learned that I am talented. I learned that I have a strong moral compass. I learned that I mattered, but sadly, this lesson was one with a lot more layers than I was prepared for.

Here I am in my early twenties, learning about myself and still looking outside of myself for gratification. Inside, I was still ugly. Inside, I was a fake and unworthy of any of the greatness life has to offer. I pushed myself to my limits and then beyond. I am a doer. I gave and gave and sought gratification from others because I was still too afraid to look inwards and find it in myself. My anxiety told me that I wasn't good enough. It told me that I couldn't be loved. It told me that the only way I would be accepted is if I killed myself doing for others. I had to prove myself to the world, and my needs were nonexistent.

I met a man. He was my best friend. We fell in love, but what we fell in love with were two versions of ourselves that were not true representations of who we genuinely were. He was hurting, and I thought I could heal the hurt if I loved him enough. I didn't see him in the way he needed to be seen, and he couldn't see me at all. I did everything I could to make him happy. I played the part. At that time, I had so many different masks that I would wear that it was extremely difficult for me to keep my roles separate. I was one person with him, and another with one friend, then another with my other friends, and so on. All of the masks and juggling being around all the different people hanging around me at the same time was exhausting, and my anxiety was through the roof. I jumped on another opportunity and started to go back to school at this point. I wanted to be a police officer and to help people. I'm a giver, right? It's what I do. I did not have any downtime. I worked, went to school, and when at home, I cleaned and cared for my love. I only stopped to sleep, and at that time, sleep was rare. I sought help to learn how to relax. A friend connected me with a physical psychologist who specialized in teaching people how to train their bodies to relax. I had not relaxed my mind or body since childhood and was at a point where I would snap if I didn't learn to control it. The tools I was given did lessen the physical response, but only temporarily. I had created a new stressor in going back to school and would only continue to build on that in the years to come.

My OCD was now making another, stronger appearance. OCD isn't only a compulsion to clean or tic. It varies for each individual, and mine is one of a compulsion to please. At my worst, not only was I counting my steps, and arriving one to two hours early for class, I was also running to catch a walk-light because it was on, and I could see it. I was in no hurry, but I was compelled to rush anyway. I'm elaborating here so you can see the state of mind I was in at the time. I was having panic attacks while doing laundry, and still, I wasn't feeling good enough and needed to *do* more. I signed onto to a role as a peace officer for a government agency in a student capacity.

This was my breaking point, and when I could no longer control any part of my mind, I started on prescription medication, but then my body started to give out on me. I was so sick. I gained a lot of weight, and was in one of the worst places, mentally, I had ever been in my life. Here was another turning point. My body was screaming at me, and I needed to make changes to survive. I stopped everything. I stopped school. Because of my health, or lack thereof, I lost my job.

I completely shifted gears. I started to look after myself again, but for all the wrong reasons. I was still seeking approval. Still trying to be someone I wasn't, and I was basing it on the needs of others. My fear of being seen as "less than" was again reinforced in that I couldn't be everything to everyone. I wasn't enough.

My partner and I had a tumultuous relationship. He came from abuse, and I was still trying to love him out of his old deep hurts. I was a victim for a long time. I put myself in a position of servitude and blamed him for it. I had no boundaries and allowed myself to be treated in a way that is, in today's society, considered to be emotionally abused, because my anxiety told me I had to (this may be triggering to some of you, but I need to share it in this way because it has taken me a long, long time, to get to this point). My mother died in a tragic accident, and my father followed her five years later. These two circumstances, though devastating, pushed me to an awareness. This awareness was that I could not depend on others for my happiness or peace of mind. I needed to take control. What if I did deserve more? What if I am needed? What if I was good enough? I had to be good enough without them there holding my hand. I had to finally see what they had seen all along—that I *am* capable, better than, actually. I found my voice. What if I ask for more? What if I demand it? I found my boundaries. I demanded change and was unwilling to accept less than what I felt I deserved, and back then, it wasn't much, but it was a start. My partner wanted to be more. He wanted to grow with me. We made changes together.

Anxiety, fear, is a powerful motivator. I have learned to control it completely. I do not experience it as I did before. I went from never being relaxed to meditating regularly and being relaxed almost exclusively. Now I use it to propel me forward. When the niggle of fear comes into my experience, I see it as a glass ceiling or a safe zone that is meant to be surpassed. I know my value and am learning to expand it every day. I know that all of the learning moments I've had in my life have led me to this place, and there is no stopping me from here. I know that I will always exceed my expectations and that my limits are only there by my making. I know that there is more in store for me, and I am excited to see what I can do.

Fear held me in captivity. It kept me submissive to my thoughts. It kept me submissive to the needs of others. It took me so far away from myself that I didn't know what was real and what was imagined. When I started to question its validity was when I started to see change. 'What if' was my savior. The next time fear tells you that you can't or that you are not good enough to deserve more, question it. What if?

Chapter

Four

Saving Yourself with a Pint of Ice Cream

By Karen Gabler

Karen Gabler

Karen Gabler is an attorney, intuitive mentor, and psychic medium. She is passionate about assisting others with a wide range of emotional and spiritual transitions, guiding them to lead their most productive and fulfilling lives. Karen works with her clients to provide intuitive guidance regarding their personal and business questions, developing strategies to help them overcome obstacles and manifest their highest purpose. She also conducts intuitive readings for clients and facilitates connections with their loved ones in spirit.

Karen is an international best-selling author and inspirational speaker. She conducts seminars and workshops on a variety of spiritual, business, and personal development topics. She taught transcendental meditation as an assistant teacher in Hawaii and legal courses as an adjunct law professor in California.

Karen earned her Bachelor of Science in psychology and her Juris Doctorate from the University of Hawaii. She is a WCIT in Martha Beck's Wayfinder Life Coach Training program and has pursued wide-ranging education in interpersonal development and the spiritual sciences, working with tutors from the prestigious Arthur Findlay College for the Psychic Sciences in England, as well as with intuitive coaches and psychic mediums throughout the United States. Karen has participated in over thirty workshops and mentorships in metaphysical topics and intuitive coaching.

Karen enjoys reading, horseback riding, and spending time with her family. You can find Karen at www.karengabler.com.

Acknowledgments:

I'd like to give a very special thanks to Brian, Sam, and Sarah. You have taught me that family is found in the heart. You have blessed me with unconditional love. You have shown me that when we are given a chance to shine our light, we can change the world. I am more grateful to you than you could ever know, and I love you more than I could ever say.

Saving Yourself with a Pint of Ice Cream
By Karen Gabler

As an intuitive mentor and coach, I regularly hear from clients who want to talk about what they have done wrong or failed to do at all. They seek guidance on how to stop themselves from engaging in conduct they have decided is "bad" for them, and then wonder why they are stuck and can't seem to make better choices.

A recurring theme of these sessions is self-condemnation for the destructive behaviors commonly used to avoid painful circumstances. Clients describe their compulsive shopping habits, substance abuse issues, food binges, or body concerns, and tell me that they are "out of control," or "have no willpower." They lament their inability to practice self-love and wonder why they keep sabotaging themselves. Like all of us, they have been taught that if we are not making the "right" choices for ourselves, we are "bad" in some way.

In advising people on how to make better self-care choices, behaviorists focus on the moment when we are about to delve into the destructive behavior, encouraging us to select a different behavior until it becomes a positive habit. Self-help enthusiasts suggest replacing deleterious choices with personal care tools such as massage, hiking, meditation, creative endeavors, and other presumably healthy and enjoyable activities. Metaphysical coaches tell us to use positive affirmations and gratitude practices to focus on manifesting the high vibrational life we desire.

While all of these practices can be useful and powerful under the right circumstances, the approach of "change your behavior, change your life" leaves many of us wondering why we simply aren't strong enough to do so. There is no question that choosing a massage or a warm bath is more productive for our physical body than binging on food or alcohol. There is also no question that taking a walk or meditating is more likely to protect our financial status than going on a shopping spree. If the positive and negative impacts of our behavioral options are so clear, why don't we make better choices? And how can we begin to do so?

The key to understanding our inability to make the "right" choices lies in noticing the judgment we place upon the "wrong" choices we've made and examining what we believe those choices say about us. We have determined (and society has confirmed) that when we engage in what we believe is "bad" behavior, instead of selecting a positive option, we are "out of control." When we make a "bad" choice, we conclude that we are hurting ourselves and have lost our capacity for self-love.

Instead, it is important to realize that the behaviors we think are hurting us are actually *helpful* to us, in their individual way. Instead of self-flagellation, we must honor our inner self for consistently taking immediate steps to protect us from pain. The reality is that *every* self-destructive behavior is essentially a courageous foray into self-care. Even the things we do that are arguably unhelpful to us are merely tools we use to survive in a moment of need. In every personal crisis, no matter how we respond, we are doing *exactly* what we need to do in that moment to take care of ourselves.

Imagine for a moment that at the end of a difficult day, you choose to self-soothe with a pint of ice cream, downing the entire container in one sitting. Conventional wisdom would tell us that this is a "bad" option. We've masked the problem, we've avoided our emotions, and we've even damaged our body. Poor choice, right? We are clearly out of control.

But before we begin the familiar cycle of self-reproach, let's look instead at what was truly going on in the middle of our ice cream binge. Were we truly out of control, or did we assume control of a painful situation? What did we actually do, and how did we genuinely feel?

In fact, what did occur is that we recognized the feeling of being in an emotional crisis and reached out, at least to ourselves. We determined that we weren't comfortable being in pain. We accepted that we wanted to feel better, and we made the choice to soothe ourselves. We knew that making our physical self feel better (at least in the moment) would soothe our hearts as well. Ultimately, we chose to take care of ourselves, as quickly and efficiently as possible.

Now, if that's true, why don't we feel better when our ice cream extravaganza is over? When the post-binge chagrin arises within us, we launch ourselves into self-degradation because we assume the behavior wasn't helpful; we lost control and made a bad choice. In fact, the behavior did exactly what we wanted it to do in that moment by providing us with comfort, joy, or relief, which is precisely what self-care should do for us.

We undermine those benefits of our self-care effort *as soon as we begin to judge that effort.* We pull ourselves out of what we assume was a foggy period of abandon, and we believe that the subsequent abuse we heap upon ourselves is our return to clarity. We insist that we must control our dangerous impulses, and we commit to keeping ourselves on track in the future—until the next time we lose control.

To alter this never-ending cycle of excess and abuse, what if we simply turn this analysis on its head? What if we recognize that the period of time in which we are binging, guzzling, or shopping is actually our moment of clarity, and the subsequent period of negativity and judgment is our fog?

We think we feel stuck because we can't stop the behavior, but actually, it is because we won't stop the subsequent self-deprecation. Instead of noting that the products we put into our bodies or the frivolous purchases we've made are hurting us (and then trying force ourselves into compliance in the future), we must remember that it is not the behaviors that are causing us pain, but instead the judgment we place on those behaviors and on ourselves.

To add insult to injury, we then tell ourselves that we deserve to be harshly judged because the behaviors we used to soothe ourselves are objectively "bad" for us. We argue that we can't merely accept the consequences of our out-of-control behavior when we already know that behavior was "bad." How can we love ourselves if our physical bodies reflect years of processed food intake with little nutritional value? How can we accept ourselves if we are riddled with debt, but keep shopping anyway? How can we trust ourselves if we continuously betray ourselves?

Altering this cycle doesn't mean that we should engage in destructive behaviors with abandon, ignoring the consequences. It doesn't mean that we should ignore the underlying issues leading to our need to self-soothe. It also does not mean that we should stop reaching for positive ways of expressing and soothing ourselves in the future. It is indisputable that when faced with a moment of personal pain, many of us could choose healthier behaviors that would give us comfort without also causing related damage to our bodies or our lives. No one would argue that eating a pint of ice cream, downing a bottle of alcohol, or going on a shopping spree you can ill afford are the best possible methods of improving your life circumstances.

That said, however, we can't have a reasonable expectation of changing those behaviors while we are still stuck—and we get stuck simply because we can't select productive self-help behaviors to provide self-care and self-love *unless and until we first reward ourselves for selecting any self-help behavior at all.* To develop self-love even in the face of clear evidence of our self-destruction, we must start by recognizing that we have demonstrated tremendous strength and courage by taking any step necessary to save ourselves from every difficult moment.

Courage is not limited to heroic acts or sheer force of will. Brené Brown said, "Courage is a heart word. The root of the word courage is cor—the Latin word for heart. In one of its earliest forms, the word courage meant 'To speak one's mind by telling all one's heart.'" This definition speaks to the level of inner strength required to be open and honest about who we are and what we need.

When we honor the choices we make by accepting those choices as our highest and best option under the circumstances presented, and we recognize the momentary healing those choices brought to our state of mind at the time, we finally begin to "tell all our heart." Most importantly, we tell it to ourselves, and we begin to develop the foundation of self-love we so dearly need instead of treating our inner selves as an enemy or obstacle to overcome.

When we acknowledge the courage and strength inherent in choosing self-preservation in every moment, instead of judging ourselves harshly for the methods used, we can begin to accept ourselves as we are, even when there are still things we might wish to change about ourselves. Robert Holden said, "Happiness and self-acceptance go hand in hand. The more self-acceptance you have, the more happiness 'you'll allow yourself to accept, receive, and enjoy.'" Self-acceptance requires that we not only recognize that we have survived the human experience, but also celebrate the profound inner growth we have achieved along the way.

Reversing decades of self-retribution takes time; be patient with yourself. Self-love must be developed gradually, much like building a muscle. Oscar Wilde said, "To love oneself is the beginning of a lifelong romance." Loving yourself is not an outcome to seek, but instead a day-by-day process of building trust in your relationship with yourself.

How do we build that relationship? To begin recognizing your purportedly destructive behaviors as self-love, stop going numb during those behaviors. To understand your needs and wants, look deeply instead of looking away. Consider the following steps:

1. Make a list of the behaviors you have used to escape or overcome a traumatic event or life stressor. Jot down examples of when you have used that behavior. What occurred in the moment that led you to the behavior? What was the behavior you used?

2. Write down how you felt when you engaged in that behavior. Ignore how you felt after it was over; skip the self-abuse and self-doubt about your choices. Instead, focus on what you felt in the moment, during the behavior itself. Did you feel relieved? Joyful? Relaxed?

3. Journal about how the behavior helped you to navigate a difficult time. Be specific and detailed. Again, ignore the aftermath, when you decided you made the wrong choice. Focus on the experience at the point where it was soothing or uplifting for you. What did that behavior do for you? How did it make you feel better about your circumstances, or about yourself?

4. Take a moment to express gratitude for the deep self-care you exercised in that moment. Write a letter to yourself, thanking your inner spirit for finding a way to address your pain, and take care of your heart. You may wish to use additional interpersonal tools such as affirmations, tapping, or meditation to solidify your gratitude for your self-care efforts.

Then, look at the thoughts and feelings you have recorded. What do they tell you about your innermost feelings, and what you need in your life to feel fulfilled and honored?

For example, when you were in the middle of eating the pint of ice cream, did you feel free to do anything that makes you happy, without the burden of arbitrary rules about what you are "allowed" to do? Did that freedom feel different from your usual life experience? If so, have you perhaps forgotten to include the exploration of new foods and flavors in your diet plan and attempted to limit yourself to a piece of fruit and a dry hamburger patty? Could you spend fifteen minutes a day finding a new recipe that would meet your nutritional goals while simultaneously exciting your palate and stimulating your brain? What else could you give back to yourself in your day-to-day life that would foster the feelings of freedom and abandon you obviously crave?

Or, when you went on a shopping spree, did you relish the idea of rewarding yourself with something completely frivolous, for no reason other than it brings you joy? Did that joy feel unusual, or perhaps even undeserved? If so, have you forgotten to reward yourself on a regular basis? Did you neglect to build joy and fun into your budget or your debt-reduction plan? Could you set aside a reasonable portion of your budget each month to buy or do something completely frivolous, simply because you want it? What else could you give back to yourself in your day-to-day life that would bring you the feelings of joy and excitement you clearly need to feed your soul?

When you stop judging your chosen behavior and instead take time to appreciate what it has done for you and how it has helped you, you begin to truly understand it and to understand yourself. It is only then that you can begin to select alternative behaviors—not because you have to, or because you should, but because you want to do so on your continued path toward self-love. This becomes possible only when you know exactly what you need and why you need it, and only after you honor your courage, strength, and resilience in overcoming the obstacles on your path.

When you recognize and respect your inherent ability to take care of yourself in each and every situation, you end the cycle of self-punishment. When you honor your inner self for protecting you in times of need, you begin to experience gratitude and love for your soul. Then, almost without even trying, you naturally begin to seek out additional self-care methods that celebrate your physical self and protect your human experience, along with allowing your inner soul to blossom.

You are the best source of knowledge about what is right for you, what makes you happy, and what you need for your inner growth. Opinions about what we should be doing or how we should be doing it are created by society, not by our souls. Glennon Doyle said, "We must bridge the gap between indoctrination and imagination. Living from the inside out, instead of from the outside in, is deep self-care." To take care of ourselves, we must honor, respect, and love all parts of ourselves. By embracing true self-care, we can experience true self-love.

Chapter

Five

The Fearless Journey
By Jaime Lee Garcia

Jaime Lee Garcia

Jaime Lee Garcia is a Certified Law of Attraction Practitioner, through the Global Sciences Foundation, since 2015, and is also studying to become certified in Belief Energy Clearing. Jaime loves to inspire others through inspirational blogs and writing, has a passion for seeing people truly happy, and aspires to teach others the law of attraction principles, which helped manifest great things into her life. Jaime would like to thank her family and friends for their constant love and support, as they bless her life in many ways. Email: secretwayoflife@yahoo.com or
Facebook @secretwayoflife.

The Fearless Journey
By Jaime Lee Garcia

"Trust in the Journey. It is when you step out of your comfort zone that you grow the most," read one of the quotes on the corkboard, which was posted at the end of the hallway of the gas station we had stopped at on our road trip. I looked up on the wall and noticed hundreds of quotes pinned to the board, as I impatiently waited for my turn to use the restroom. I love writing inspirational blogs and quotes, so the notes caught my attention. Some were quotes I have read before, but the new ones made me ponder.

As I read that first quote, memories flooded my mind of the day I took the biggest leap of faith and jumped miles out of my comfort zone. Conquering fear of the unknown and what it would mean for my future was unsettling, as I had to find the courage to make a big life-altering decision. This decision was something I was not sure I could do at the time. It meant leaving my daughters, along with everyone and everything I had ever known, and moving across the country to start a life with the man I had fallen in love with. This was the most difficult decision to make and quite frankly scared the death out of me.

Nine months before this life-changing move, I had reconnected with a guy from high school on Facebook. We were great friends back in school, but nothing more. So, the instant connection over the phone hit me by surprise, especially since he was now living across the country from me. The last time we had seen each other, we were only twenty years old. He had joined the Army and was headed for Germany. Life took us both on different paths at that time, and we never spoke again until we were 42 years old. We both had been married for many years and were newly single with two daughters. Within two months of talking on the phone, we began flying back and forth to see each other. Only four months after reconnecting, he dropped to one knee and proposed at the airport during one of my trips to see him. He was dead set against moving back to California, where both of our parents and I lived. To be together, it meant I had to make the greatest sacrifice and leave everyone and everything behind, except for my youngest daughter, who had promised to come with me for one year. This move across the country meant that I had to find serious courage to let go of the life I had always known and start a new one, in a strange place that I had never been to, without knowing a soul, and without my familiar tribe near me.

Being the youngest daughter, I was always glued to my parent's hips and loved spending time with them. When I had my two daughters, we spent every weekend with my parents going to lunches, dinners, movies, making crafts together, taking drives to see extended family, and so forth. Holidays with extended family were always a big deal, planned six months in advance, and filled with so much fun and memory-making. Life was always about family to me, and I never fathomed in my wildest dreams of ever living more than a city away from them. While raising my two daughters, my parents always lived close. Twice, they even lived on the same street as us. Getting married the first time at the age of 19 meant that I greatly depended on them to help me navigate through married life and motherhood. Having them close was also a source of security for me.

Being a sensitive soul, it became harder each day as the time approached to pack the Penske truck and head on the journey to my new home. A lot of tears had flowed as I began to think about all the goodbyes I would have to say before leaving. I honestly did not know how I would be able to say goodbye to my oldest daughter, my parents, brother, niece, extended family, and all my best and dearest friends. I had to pray a lot and manifest an emotionally smooth transition for this new journey, my happiness, and my well-being.

I will share with you in this chapter, how I overcame the fear of this journey, in hopes that it will help you during times when you feel you are in unchartered territory, or when fear seems to be holding you back from fulfilling your dreams. As you may know by now, life is filled with many situations in which we must overcome fear and find the courage to make the most difficult decisions to better our lives or to grow in some ways. We have all experienced fear when starting a new job, moving to a new home, walking down the aisle on our wedding day, and giving birth for the first time, to name a few. If you remember back to some of these moments, you can smile, knowing that you made it through. You are here, and you learned valuable lessons along the way. Sometimes, we find the fear we carried was unwarranted and that we worried for no reason. Other times, fear seemed to be validated.

As a law of attraction practitioner, and studying to become certified in Belief Energy Clearing, I have had to tap into my learned techniques to get through my fears. I know that fear will appear in many instances in my life, such as with my life-changing move across the country, but I now have the measures in my pocket to help me face them with positivity and confidence. After reading this chapter, I hope you can also take away some techniques in which to help you find courage when faced with challenging situations.

Many people ask me, "What exactly is the law of attraction, and what can it mean for me?" There are 12 universal laws, and the law of attraction is the seventh. It can basically be defined as follows: "How we create the things, events, and people that come into our lives. Our thoughts, feelings, words, and actions produce energies, which, in turn, attract like energies. Simply put, negative thoughts attract negative thoughts and positive thoughts attract positive thoughts. "Think of the most basic law of physics—the law of gravity. When an apple sways in the wind and is detached from a branch, an invisible force (gravity) pulls it down to the ground at a precise speed. This happens each time as gravity performs its sole function effortlessly. You can feel gravity, but you cannot see it. It cannot be heard, nor can it be touched, but you are aware that gravity is there because it is with you when you run, walk, drive your car, or perform bungee jumping off of a cliff. The law of attraction works in the same way. It is there whether you like it or not. It takes thought and focus to make the law work for you, but it can be used by anyone to manifest great things into your life and to gain courage when needed if you understand how to properly apply its principles.

The first lesson is to understand that whatever you are focusing on and putting your energy into, the law will bring more of that into your life, good or bad. It does not discriminate. Have you ever said to yourself, "I am not feeling great, and I cannot get sick," only to get more ill by the minute? That is because you were focusing on *sickness* and not on good health. What you were actually doing was manifesting more sickness to deal with. Instead, you might have said, "I am feeling better by the minute. My health is great!" With that in mind, if you focus on your fears, more situations in which to worry about will come your way. So, make sure to do away with worry, fear, anger—any emotion of negativity. This would be the wrong frequency to be on when we are trying to attract great events into our lives. Re-train your brain to focus on the positive only, even the smallest of things to be grateful for. You have probably heard people throughout your lifetime mention, "Remember to say your daily affirmations!" This statement could not be truer to change your life for the better and to get rid of fear.

A month before my big move across the country, life was extremely busy with packing up my house and preparing to move to my new home in Kentucky, on top of working full time. I had spent my entire life living in California, with family and friends always within arm's reach. Moving to a new state that I had never even visited was unnerving. I tried to tuck away my emotions for most of that last month, spending time with everyone I loved as much as possible. Keeping busy kept my mind off the reality of how life-altering my decision to move was.

From the moment Christopher and I fell in love, everything happened so quickly. I felt like I was being guided by some invisible force, almost like I was watching everything play out from the clouds. The moment was surreal. One day, however, I had an epiphany and had to laugh at myself, as the reality was that I had manifested the whole reconnection with Christopher. While newly single for the first time since I was 19, I found myself in unchartered territory. I was being taken out on dates with guys that I had known in some capacity over the years. However, I did not like being single. I was always a committed kind of girl and did not want to date at all. Having recently learned about the law of attraction and remembering how it worked on my life in amazing ways, I set out to manifest my true love and put out the intention. The day I told a friend that I wanted to wait for my soulmate and would know who he was by the connection we would instantly have, is the exact day that Christopher had called out of the blue. We had not physically talked since we were 20 years old. After our four-hour phone call that night, reconnecting, I knew that my soulmate had come into my life the same day I had asked the universe for him. Everything took off from there in rapid speed.

The week of my move is when everything seemed to hit me all at once. Although I had the full support of my family and friends, all I could do was focus on how sad I felt about leaving everything and everyone behind. I felt insecure about being in a different state and not knowing how to get anywhere. Even though I had always been a people-person and made friends easily throughout my life, I was frightened that I would not fit in with the people in my new small town. Having been at the same job for years, I was also unsure of starting a new career and not having time off to go visit my family frequently. I knew all these feelings were only natural; however, I could not stop the sadness and was making myself a bit of a mess. One particular evening, I sat on the edge of the bed while wiping away tears that would not stop flowing when the corner of a book sitting on the top of a moving box caught my eye. It was the first book I had ever read, regarding the law of attraction, and it was this book that had changed my life a couple of years prior. It was those principles that brought Christopher and me together.

I then realized that I was focusing on sadness and loss and was completely on the wrong frequency. To make this an easier transition for myself and my family, I had to immediately change my thoughts and get on a positive frequency. Otherwise, I knew I would not make it through this life change. I began setting out to change my thought process and put aside all fears to focus on positive events to take place. Remembering the basic principles of the power of intent, I focused on everything positive I could imagine about the move, such as the following:

- “This move will be the best decision for me at this point in my life.”
- “Christopher and I will have an amazing life together.”
- “My life will be filled with many new adventures, and I will get to see areas of the country I have never been to.”
- “I will be able to continue working remotely for my boss, which will give me the flexibility to come home to California and see my kids frequently.”
- “I will meet new and interesting people that will enrich my life in many ways.”
- “My kids will have somewhere to travel to when they need a reprieve from their busy lives.”

I said these affirmations every day until it was time to pack up the moving truck and caravan to my new home. Although the goodbyes were extremely hard, I focused only on the positive things that were to come my way. Now, seven years later, I can honestly say that my life has been everything verbalized in those affirmations. Focusing on the positive manifested more wonderful things into my life, which I feel so blessed for. I do work remotely for my boss in California, which gives me the flexibility to fly back and forth and spend precious time with my family and friends. Christopher and I spend our days off on adventurous road trips, traveling to new places frequently, which is my favorite thing to do. When I let go of my fears, my life transformed, and it can happen for you too.

Remember, you are who you believe and think of yourself to be. Therefore, never think of yourself as a victim because you are not one. Do not even let that word exist in your mental dictionary. Instead, believe yourself to be a survivor, a victor, and you will persevere through anything because you indeed have a courageous heart. Life is filled with challenges and tragedies, but it is also filled with love, joy, life lessons, and amazing, magical moments. When a situation is calling for your courage, practice your daily positive affirmations, and always know with your entire core, that you are a warrior who can and will conquer anything headed your way. Always remember your many blessings, and always remember to “shine on” my friends!

Chapter

Six

Above All, Honor Yourself
By Sara Hamblin

Sara Hamblin

Sara is an energy worker, channeler, and Reiki Master. She helps individuals work through energetic blocks that have occurred in their bodies due to emotional trauma and other life events. She is able to accomplish this through her training and personal experience in using energy work to heal from grief on a physical and subconscious level. Her purpose is to help people heal on a soul level so they can live life fully. You can reach Sara at sara@moonworks.energy or at www.moonworks.energy.

Above All, Honor Yourself
By Sara Hamblin

For the last few months, I spent days staring at a blank page in my mind. I contributed to our previous book, *The Grateful Soul*, and spent hours pouring my heart onto the page. During the process, tears flowed freely, would stop, then would flow again. I concisely put years of my grief and pain onto the page in a beautiful letter to death. Death brought me to a deep place of gratitude. Now, it was time to take on courage. Courage didn't feel the same as gratitude. Gratitude resembled a peaceful willow tree. Courage resembled a lion. I couldn't put the ferocity and courage I felt into words on a page. At the time, my life seemed to be going well. I had a job in the midst of the lockdown because of Covid-19, my social life was thriving thanks to technology, but I still had a sense of uneasiness.

My boyfriend and I celebrated two years of being together in mid-April when the lockdown was in full swing. It should have been a major milestone—it was his longest relationship to date and my first successful committed relationship after my divorce three years ago. But somehow, I wasn't the kind of happy I thought I'd be. Our relationship was strangely silent. There was a wall being built between us that neither of us talked about. On the outside, I was a strong proponent of honoring the divine feminine and divine masculine, doing energy work, and working on deep healing within myself that the universe would be proud of. But when I was at home, I was missing the mark. Badly.

I was terrified to ask my friends and spirit guides about the future of my relationship. I didn't want to hear the inevitable truth. But as I reflected, it became apparent. We had moved in together after a month and a half of dating so I could escape a psychologically damaging living situation that involved a neighbor and borderline legal action. Rather than giving most of my paycheck over to rental and move-in costs at an apartment complex in the heart of Denver, I accepted my boyfriend's offer of living together for a fraction of the price. We hardly knew each other at that point, and I figured we'd quickly realize whether the relationship would last. I didn't have to sign a lease or pay a deposit, and he was willing to watch my dogs while I traveled extensively for work. It seemed ideal. Since I was traveling two to three weeks of every month, I didn't pay much attention to the resistance and resentment that slowly started to build. I thought the issues were small enough they'd resolve themselves.

The second year of our relationship was difficult. The honeymoon phase wore off, and the hopes and dreams we'd communicated early on seemed to be getting further away. Each time we tried approaching a difficult topic, it seemed to end in a way that was unresolved and left an awkward silence. I found myself compromising my desires and waiting until he was ready to take on something new, like a potential business partnership, and I continued pursuing activities he didn't take an interest in. I saw his potential, and I kept waiting for him to magically show up as the person I felt he could be. The relationship seemed okay, and right before our two-year anniversary, we celebrated my birthday in the mountains as a last hurrah before the Coronavirus turned off the world for a few months. When the official stay-at-home orders were put in place, I was not prepared for the microscope that was placed on everything we'd been avoiding.

The first few weeks of the lockdown were blissful. We splurged on a Nintendo Switch and drove forty-five minutes out of the way to pick it up before stores began shutting off to the world. After working remotely during the day, we'd spent our evenings laughing and playing hours of video games, reliving a new version of our childhood fantasies. We drank wine and did Bob Ross paintings by watching old episodes on YouTube. We made mimosa brunches on the weekends and spent the afternoons listening to friends perform concerts on Facebook Live. We did a good job of ignoring the important conversations we never finished. There was no need to ruin the fun, playful vibe. Then, we contracted the virus.

My boyfriend showed symptoms first, with a mild fever and a strange cough. The day after, I started showing symptoms as well, which included a complete loss of taste and smell. Within a day of the initial onset, we were both bedridden. It was difficult to go up the stairs, and we felt constantly tired and out of breath. Our symptoms only lasted a few weeks, but this was a new level of isolation to protect others from what we had experienced. My boyfriend had mild symptoms that carried on for a few weeks after mine had subsided. We continued to quarantine ourselves to minimize any contact with the outside world until we had both been symptom-free for two weeks.

When you spend every minute of your day with another person, you pay attention to the things you ignore. Small situations that were previously only slightly irritating can become monumental issues. Conversations that were never resolved begin to resurface. What was once your home and safe haven becomes an incubator for everything that no longer works in your relationship. As issues continued to surface, I knew I had to make a choice. I could honor myself and stick to my truth, or I could surrender and stop asking for what I desired in both our partnership and our relationship. Every relationship prior had been an exercise in how to keep the other person comfortable, happy, and feeling secure. What about me? What about the desires I consistently chose to forego because there wasn't space in the relationship for them? What about my hopes and dreams for myself and our partnership? I came to a head with myself. I could compromise myself again, or I could honor myself by continuing to ask for what I needed and desired from my life and my partner. I chose to honor myself. He chose to end our relationship.

During the six months leading up to this point, I was in a period of rapid transformation. I had put my healing and personal development into overdrive, and nothing and no one was going to stop me. I was connecting with my inner self in a way that I didn't know was possible. I had received a glimpse of my true north, and I was going to continue moving in that direction at all costs. I knew I was here to help heal people in the world, but I struggled to have this exist while being in our relationship due to the demands and double duty of managing a full-time job as well. I felt alive for the first time in a long time, and I wanted my relationship to work. I adored the man I was with, and I spent a year trying to course-correct what felt like a slowly derailing freight train. Based on our conversations leading up to that point, I had to pick where my allegiance would lie. It was either choosing myself and my truth or choosing to compromise once again for the relationship. I had spent over ten years of my life in committed relationships with other people I had compromised myself for. As I reflected on the years and lessons, I had to ask myself—where was my commitment to myself? I hadn't done a good job of being committed to myself, and I knew I'd have to consciously choose.

Choosing yourself can be difficult when you've spent your entire life serving other people. Everyone else came first--always. Their issues took priority, my problems weren't that big. Their comfort always came first; I can go along with whatever the other person wants to do. I was terrified of saying the wrong thing—what if I offend them or they disagreed? What if they don't like me because of what I feel or say? I became comfortable placing myself into a tiny box, so I didn't rock the boat. I wanted to go with the flow, and I made it my responsibility to make sure everyone else was happy, loved, and secure. But when I finally stopped and looked at who I'd become, I didn't recognize anything about myself. Who was I? Who was I without everything I did for other people? Who was I for me?

The last three months have been a process of disentangling from the old version of myself. This takes immense courage. I began confronting my fears, traumatic experiences, and entire being that kept me in toxic and cyclical patterns. I sat with my shadows so I could see, and so I could understand.

Who was I in the darkness of my soul? Why did I need to be needed so badly? I found that our souls are never as dark as we think they are. As I opened up and shared, my darkness didn't seem so dark. I wanted to release everything that no longer served me. I didn't want to be needed or question who I was without the love of others. I decided to become an example for others of what is possible through deep, soul-level healing. I had three teachers guiding me in various aspects of intuition and listening to my inner truth, healing my chakras, and learning the ins and outs of traditional shamanism. I wanted to heal myself, so I could help guide others in their healing.

Healing can be a difficult and unsettling experience. You begin to reopen your old wounds—some that you've had for decades—and begin to scrape out all of the energetic crap that has been hanging around. It is raw, vulnerable, and liberating. For years, I held my wounds with shame and embarrassment. I was terrified to open them up to anyone. What would they think of me? If I showed my wounds to those I said I loved and trusted, would they still accept me? Would they still love me? Would they still want and need me? By hiding what I was experiencing, I thought I was keeping myself protected and safe. I now see that it was the energetic equivalent of wrapping a bandage tightly around an open cut, never letting it breathe, never changing the bandage, and never cleaning out the wound. Doing this causes infections. When we withhold sharing in a healing space, we don't allow others to contribute to our healing. We think we know best, and we don't need help from anyone else. I chose to hide my wounds for a long time. And they festered. They manifested in damaging ways. For years, I had an unhealthy relationship with alcohol, men, and myself. It took months of soul searching and a difficult bout with sobriety to open up. I realized that I was not the issue. My wounds were not the issue. My need to be needed was not the issue. I kept tuning into the programming that ran my life for years. But this time, I realized it was programming that no longer worked.

One day I realized how far my inner work had brought me. I audibly heard my guides say, "We interrupt your regularly-scheduled programming to bring you this breaking news." It was the perfect analogy for the work I was doing and the work I was leading others in as well. An interruption in my normal programming was exactly what I needed. I needed it for myself and for others. If I was going to become the best version of myself, I knew I had to change what I was doing. When I looked at my alignment with the highest and best version of myself, I was not on track. I was not honoring myself. It's as if I was not a part of the same conversation. The breaking news was that I was not aligned with where I was meant to be, and if I was going to be the best version of myself, I needed a massive overhaul. And to make this overhaul happen, I had to make a conscious decision to step into courage every day.

Courage is staring into the darkness of the unknown and stepping into it anyway. It's feeling around in the darkness of an unfamiliar room until you find a wall or a light switch. It's sitting with the anxiety and fear, and not choosing the familiarity and comfort because you know it no longer serves you. In the days after our official split, I reached out to my community. I'd never had a community I chose to rely on. When I reached out and asked for help in the darkness, everyone I loved, and that loved me showed up with a candle to light the way. They fed me, loved me, offered me a place to stay, and cared for my dog, so I could travel. The day I decided to move, I had five friends show up to help me temporarily pack up my life and put it into storage. I have never seen a fully packed fifteen-foot U-Haul unloaded in fifteen minutes, but these beautiful souls made it happen in a space filled with love and joy. And they agreed to come and do it again in the future when I received the keys to my permanent residence. Courage is asking for what you need when you need it—and allowing it to show up for you.

As I sit in the midst of this life transformation, I find myself on another beautiful adventure because I allowed myself to step into the unknown. I'm staring out from the back of a 48-foot catamaran with eight beautiful humans who were strangers and acquaintances two weeks ago. We spent twelve days sailing around Puerto Rico and hours digging deep into our souls to see where we are holding ourselves back. What are we capable of? Who are we on a soul level? Who are we as individuals and as a collective? By having courage, trust, and openness to authenticity, I allowed eight mirrors to see me, show me who I am, and fill me with love and acceptance. Not only have I found my soul family, I see my true north and where I am going. I am here to help, to heal, and to love fully. There is nothing to do except love and be loved in return. Courage is being presented with a life-changing opportunity and stepping into it fully with everything you are.

Chapter

Seven

My Journey Through the Heart
By Dr. Vicki L. High

Dr. Vicki L. High

Dr. Vicki L. High is an international, multiple-best-selling author, life coach, counselor, speaker, founder of Heart 2 Heart Healing, Reiki Master Teacher, and former mayor. Her books include *Heart 2 Heart Connections: Miracles All Around Us*, and is a contributing author to *When I Rise, I Thrive*, *Healer*, *Life Coach*, *Inspirations*, *When Angels Speak*, *Holistic*, and *Manifestations*. Dr. High boldly journeys as a pioneer in holistic healing, counseling, empowerment, and spirituality. She connects ideas and concepts, creating patterns for coaching and healing. She teaches people how to practice Heart 2 Heart Healing, to live

authentically, and to courageously dump baggage in an inspired, powerful method—*Mini-Me* and *Draining Relationship* exercises. Contact her at Vhigh4444@aol.com; www.heart2heartconnections.us;
FB: @heart2heartprograms; @ce2oinc; @drvickilhigh; @kalmingkids; and @empowereddreams.

Acknowledgments

I want to acknowledge the power of unconditional love as a catalyst for change. My grateful thanks to friends and family who enrich my life and the people who have touched my life in extraordinary ways. Special thanks to Diane Sellers, Tina and Lon Morgan, Dorothy Oliver, Rev. Pat Moore and her husband, Rev. Glenn Moore, Darlene Owen, Jamie Norman, Janene Cates

I am sad to say that Dr. Vicki L. High passed away this year. We remain devastated by this loss but understand, as you will after reading her chapter, how needed she is on the other side. She made our lives better in the author community. Everyone who she touched in life has been transformed by her kindness, generosity and healing spirit. We are universally held by her now and always. – Kyra Schaefer, As You Wish Publishing

My Journey Through the Heart
By Dr. Vicki L. High

In 2005, my good friend asked if I would teach a Heart 2 Heart Healing Practitioners Workshop at her church near Waco, Texas. I felt slightly uneasy. Church? My heart was rather bruised from trying to share my miraculous experiences with members of church communities. One minister turned his head away from me and stopped mid-sentence, ending our conversation abruptly, when I tried to share the miraculous healing work I had witnessed.

Despite my trepidation, it has always been a blessing to share the wonder and excitement of things happening to people in sessions and workshops. I was excited about scheduling the event. We set a date and prepared for the small, intimate experience. Spirit always seems to manage the guest list. People arrive as strangers and leave the end of the workshop as family, but in this workshop, they were already church family.

The workshop was exciting, and there were many memorable moments, but one remained with me years later. In that session, one participant shared that she journeyed beyond the room and found herself standing before a group—a "council of people." They sat in a semi-circle, and she stood before them, answering their queries. She described their apparel, their uniforms, as burgundy with white triangular chest insets from shoulders to abdomen.

There was an insignia embroidered across white cuffs on the sleeves. She said they looked similar, but not exactly like Asian designs. As she spoke, I recalled a book with a specific picture in it that matched her description. I pulled the book from my portable library and turned to the referenced page to show her. Her eyebrows went up as she exclaimed, "Yes, they looked exactly like that!"

In the days prior to the event with the church group, I was also asked to deliver the message during Sunday service. As a relatively new minister, my work was focused more on healing than in speaking to congregations, but I was happy to serve. After we completed the workshop, I knew I had to work on my message for the church service the next morning. I poured through my thoughts, wrote volumes of detailed notes, and marked passages from references that supported what I had to say. I wanted to honor the people listening and spirit, who guided my thoughts. My desire was to provide a message of love, unconditional love. I was both nervous and excited. I was also prepared to the best of my ability. I stepped up to the podium, and I placed my notes and book there to use.

Most of my life, I have been aware of my connection to God and Jesus. I have an ongoing conversation with them. As people share experiences, I often hear additional information that comes through simultaneously. It is as if a stream of "conscious knowing" is added to what I hear, feel, and see. I have always trusted it and known it as truth. I experience it as a deliberate, declarative sentence or thought. This gift has grown stronger as I practice and teach Heart 2 Heart Healing.

From the podium, I took a deep breath. I looked out over the congregation, connected to my sacred heart, and opened my mouth to speak. Then, something miraculous happened! The words that poured out were not mine. For the next thirty minutes, words continued to flow from me, but they were not taken from the notes I so diligently prepared. I cannot tell you what I said because the words did not come from the place in my brain where I had recall or memory of those words. I completed the message without opening the book or looking at my notes.

I have an ongoing agreement with Jesus that he can speak through me anytime he wishes. I knew he had decided to do so on that Sunday morning in April. If I had said that to anyone, I know they would have thought, "Sure. Is she nuts?" No one was more surprised than me when we reached the end of the message and, "Do you have any questions?" came out of my mouth. I never heard a minister complete the message offering a Q & A for the congregation! Jesus answered questions that people asked. When I asked for a copy of the recorded message, the church technician said there was a problem with the recording. There was no tape of the message available.

The next day I was providing Heart 2 Heart Healing sessions for the people who scheduled appointments. One man, when I asked for feedback, let me know at the end of the session, that he had come face-to-face with Jesus—literally. He said, "Jesus was in my face! His face was right here!" He placed his hand with extended fingers less than an inch from his face. "Until now, I'd never have admitted something like that!" Then, he offered his gift to me when he said, "Oh, by the way. You know, you weren't the one speaking yesterday.

It was him." I acknowledged his insight and, with a smile, said, "Yes, you're right. It was him."

Another time, I attended a conference in Phoenix, Arizona. A woman asked a question about political lobbies. Since I was a former mayor, I wanted to speak with her further about her question. I also wanted an autograph from an author whose book I had brought. I had to choose between talking with the woman or having my book signed. I chose the autograph. I realized I was a little disappointed that I had lost my opportunity to speak about the lobbies. I picked up my lunch and greeted people seated at a random table, as I joined them. I sat down, I looked to my right, and there she was, the woman with the question about political lobbies. I had been given a second chance to speak and learn about her mission. We visited for a long while, and she later came to visit me in Texas.

We spent the weekend with her learning how to become a Heart 2 Heart Healing Practitioner. Right before it was time to take her back to the airport, I heard the question in my heart, "Why don't you ask if she would like to exchange sessions?" Our Heart 2 Heart Healing lessons had concluded, but this was just an exchange from practitioner to practitioner. She agreed, and we began the sessions.

I am truly blessed and honored to say Jesus has visited with me on several occasions. He is not the guy who still hangs upon the cross in some churches, and he is not the same person who I learned about in Sunday school. He is real, loving, and tells me that there is more to his story than we know from two thousand years ago. One thing I know for sure is that he is still orchestrating and attending events, and I am exceedingly willing to join him for these excursions.

During her session with me, I started feeling tears flowing, first from my left eye and then my right eye. That is my sign for Jesus' presence when he shows up in my sessions, and I felt him in the healing room. My session was experiential and peaceful. He said to me, "You've asked for help. Here it is. Relax into this." He commented, "Every person you've done a healing [session] on, you've changed their lives. Every workshop you've given, you've changed their lives. You are so loved. You have no idea of the changes you've already made in the world." There's something extra special about Jesus delivering that message to me. He also shared these words, "Wherever you walk, I walk. Whoever you love, I love." He then repeated the verse, "Come unto me all who are heavy laden, and I will give you rest. Take your yoke upon me and learn of me, for I am meek and lowly of heart, and you shall find rest unto your soul." Then in a flash, he was a modern version of himself and said, "You've got this!" Then he said, "We've got this!" That is when I smiled. He truly is funny, but we do not often get to experience that part of him. When he was here, I was unaware of anything or anyone else in the room. I was totally focused on him and the experience of being with him."

This work is not for the faint of heart. It takes a courageous heart to continue to share miracles with people. In the beginning, due to fearful criticism and walls of resistance, I tiptoed while sharing the message. My reticence did not change the miracles or my wonder at what happened. Through the years, change has been reflected in the growing numbers of people now ready to listen. I still walked quietly, but gathered more information and experiences, becoming a credible eyewitness to the marvelous works of God. I watched people transform their lives through miracles of new birth, even though these hopeful parents had been told they would never have children. I loved hearing doctors say, "I can't explain this," as healing miracles changed the prognoses in dozens of desperate situations. The spiritual enlightenment and encounters with heavenly beings changed my life and the lives of witnesses who were there with me when these experiences exploded the belief boxes that contained the lessons from my childhood and the church. Today, I walk humbly with firm and decisive steps in honor and service of the magnificent *All That Is*. Unconditional love, the most powerful force in the Universe, transforms everything. I consider myself one of the luckiest people on the planet to be gifted with this assignment. My job is to share that this gift of Heart 2 Heart unconditional love is equally available to each of us who have "ears to hear."

In the Heart 2 Heart Healing work, we learn how to activate our sacred hearts. We speak about the physical heart, the energetic heart—also known as the heart chakra—and the sacred heart. My sacred heart is my umbilical cord, my personal holy of holies, that connects me directly to the heart and mind of God. My spiritual journey has taken my simple country road and expanded it into a superhighway. My goal as a human, in my opinion, is to become more aware of God's existence and presence in my life. I had to let go of my restrictive, limiting beliefs before I could become open to miracles. As I acknowledge God within me, I become filled with unconditional love and light. That empowers me to recognize that unconditional love and light in others.

When I allow unconditional love to freely flow from source, then my life is changed. I am more compassionate, and I show more loving kindness to those who are struggling in a world that is not always supportive during times of stress.

Each of us has the power to choose a different path, transforming pain into joy, challenge into change, and stress into laughter. Sometimes when we are stressed to our limits, it is difficult to see how anything can change our situations. With unconditional love, we have the greatest catalyst for change at our disposal. We always have the power of choice. We can decide to tap into the power to move from anger to joy, to engage in the dance, and add new steps, so we can powerfully journey along a new path, find our balance and live in peace, or we can choose to be a victim of our feelings.

Each day presents more opportunities to act from the power of a courageous heart—to do what is right, to do what is loving, and to do what comes straight from the heart. Dictionaries show the original meaning of courage is derived from the French word meaning heart, and they also show this definition is now obsolete. I wonder who decided that! It means a courageous heart is actually an oxymoron, but I love it: Heart [2] Heart!

Chapter *Eight*

The Courage to Stay Awake

By Rosemary Hurwitz

Rosemary Hurwitz

Rosemary Hurwitz, a married mom of four young adults, is passionate about an inner-directed life, and she found the focus for it in the Enneagram. She has coached with and taught the Enneagram for 18 years. The Enneagram is a time-honored personality to higher consciousness and well-being paradigm.

She gives Enneagram-based individual coaching for deepened awareness, better relationships, emotional wellness, and deeper spiritual connection. Rosemary has certifications in intuitive counseling and angel card reading, and uses these wisdom traditions in her spiritual teaching and coaching. For twenty-five years, along with her husband, Dale, she gave Discovery Weekend retreats, patterned after Marriage Encounter, for engaged couples.

She is an accredited professional member of the International Enneagram Association and will be presenting at their 2020 conference on using the Enneagram to set healthy boundaries. Rosemary has taught internationally and has been published in nine inspirational compilation books, including, *No Mistakes, How You Can Change Adversity into Abundance.* Her first single-authored, best-selling book is, *Who You Are Meant To Be: The Enneagram Effect.* Connect with her at www.spiritdrivenliving.com. Book reviews: https://bit.ly/theenneagrameffect.

The Courage To Stay Awake
By Rosemary Hurwitz

It is so much easier to sink my teeth into a toasted English muffin with all the nooks and crannies, sip my coffee and write my daily to-do list than listen to the difficult morning news.

The news of the day is the Black Lives Matter movement, including protests and rioting following the killing of George Floyd by a Minneapolis police officer. There is also pandemic news of Covid-19 cases spiking after varying degrees of reopening the economy and the upcoming 2020 presidential election. Anxiety seems high.

I have felt like the low notes on the piano for several days now, and yet, I know it isn't time for a pity party. I am a firm believer in "feel it to heal it," so I am also committed to naming and feeling the entire span of notes I am feeling, whatever they may be. When I would prefer to distract myself or stick my head in the sand, I know that the easiest way out is through, and forge through this difficult time I will.

Naming the feelings is first. My heart cries out for deepened awareness and compassion for all of us, including those who lead us. It cries out for those of us (that would be all of us) who need to be better led. My heart cries out in this ending of the spring season, which has had enough losses and grist for the mill, it seems, to last one's lifetime.

I am aware that I am not alone in my sadness or frustration as the champagne of seasons approaches, which helps somewhat. It seems that we wait for summertime, forever, in the Midwest, so I will not miss it, and it does help to know we are all feeling similar shades of grief and are certainly not alone in this crisis. There is a kind of safety in numbers. Giving myself all the good advice I'd give to my clients and students, I say to myself, "Let yourself grieve these losses, of deaths lost to the Coronavirus and to the virus of systemic racism. Let yourself feel this pain, like the labor pains of childbirth that will ultimately push out a new life."

Along with the sadness and grief, I feel gratitude too. I am grateful that no family or close friends have gotten the Coronavirus, and that we are figuring out how to get a pandemic under control in our world even if it is "forward three steps, back two." That the world is going through a pandemic together is amazing in itself.

I am grateful to these sacrificial lambs like George Floyd, who so sadly seemingly had to die for the rest of us to wake up even more than we were before. I know that in crises when we are all on our knees, is when, with perspective and time, leaps of growth can be felt. Otherwise, it seems we only take baby steps to grow.

My heart cries out, but it is with staying awake and keeping the faith of the big picture, that it is relieved at times, of its pain. It is in this place where I bless the day and the night, the light and the shadow, and keep faith in the dark nights of the soul that I find meaning.

I believe in a God and a source that enters into the challenges with us, with all of my aligned body mind and spirit. The

Dali Lama clearly states the importance of hope as well, in this Tibetan truism: "Tragedy should be utilized as a source of strength no matter what the difficulties, or how painful the experience is. If we lose our hope, that is the real disaster."

I was wondering about the metaphor, "It is often darkest before the dawn," and how it relates to staying awake. This metaphor is the ultimate expression of what it means to be faithful. It speaks to our most difficult moments, coming right before a new level of consciousness and a new energy enters within us. Within experiences like a pandemic, we can have a collective consciousness upgrade, with perspective, so to speak. What can that look like? More respect and willingness to do the inner work toward wellness, and not simply to talk of it, may be one gift that arises from illness and death. As we reach its third month, the pandemic has taught me like nothing else has, how we are responsible for each other.

So, if these challenges are happening *for* us, not *to* us, there is a gift in this somewhere. There must be a gift in this experience of mass illness and loss of lives during a pandemic. There will be a gift in the loss of black and brown lives due to systemic racism in our police departments and beyond. There will be multiple gifts if we know how to look for them. Maybe staying awake is asking for the guidance and then trusting ourselves to put one foot in front of the other. There is a saying going around social media, about courage, and I am paraphrasing, but it is about courage and how having courage does not always look like a big roar. Sometimes courage is merely getting through another day. Rather, courage is being patient and faithful that there will be guidance and keeping the faith that all suffering will not go in vain.

When people were saying or questioning on general media that we were back to the 1960s with the raging racism and rioting that follows in crises, I disagreed. If it were true, then it would mean we didn't learn anything from Martin Luther King, Jr., or from John Kennedy or Robert Kennedy or Rosa Parks or Maya Angelou or so many others who helped us move partially up the mountain. These leaders and many others, helped us see that equal and different is sacred. If you are not spiritually inclined, then you can look at claiming diversity as a way to achieve harmony and peace in this life. Like all of the parts of the body that are working together in exquisite and individual paths toward healing, we can work together in harmony—equal and different.

Diversity would not have been celebrated by so many of us if we had learned nothing since the 1960s. In my prayer, so many people, white, black, and brown, are needed to see the sacredness of diversity, to celebrate it.

Giant leaps for humanity driven by the spirit take so much patience and perseverance. Psychologically speaking, the same polarities that run through a society's tapestry and politics of shadow and light, have their foundation in the human beings that make up that society.

The polarities of shadow and light will continue to run through the human being forever. That is the foundation for our creative force. And, it is how we accept this dynamic within the human condition, and to what degree we practice self-awareness, and self-acceptance, and understand the gifts in our shadow, that these polarities can be diminished.

In that merciful place where we have deep compassion for ourselves and each other, we will offer and be offered greater peace than we have ever known.

Being patient through the difficult times of unrest and asking for guidance can bring about periods of new awareness, which is so needed. So can calls to action. In the Black Lives Matter movement, listening to the heartbreaking daily stories of a black or brown person who was bullied for no reason can be so helpful. I believe listening to their stories can support us all. From someone who admits to being raised by blatant racists to those of us who had liberal professors for fathers, all of us have strains of racism if we lived in a racist society or culture.

We must examine the range of racism from quiet to raging attitudes. Even people who don't think they have any tendencies might check the subtle racist attitudes in their hearts and homes.

It is the responsibility of each of us to become extra aware. How did subtle racist attitudes permeate the environment in which we lived? That question is a wonderful place to start with our reawakening. Here are a few examples from my life. I recently was in a discussion regarding subtle or seemingly smaller ways that racism affected me.

There is a suburban moms group on Facebook I am part of that talks about the impact still felt from the 1960s. The story goes that in our village, instead of developing a low-income housing development for minority groups, the district went ahead with a new park with several amenities for this already affluent town.

In other words, instead of sharing the wealth, we hoarded it. Instead of aligning with the sacredness of diversity, we subtly dissed it, under the guise of the "village's needs." I didn't do this, but I live here, and the good news is there is always a time for new growth under Heaven. At this time in June of 2020, renaming a park to honor the first black family, who had the courage to stay awake and know their worth, is about to happen. Someone who started this renaming of the park to honor the Black Lives Matter movement said, "I know this is a small thing but—" I replied, "Not at all, remember Mother Teresa said, 'Do little things with great love.' Margaret Mead's famous quote is, 'Never doubt that a small group of thoughtful citizens can change the world. Indeed, it is the only thing that ever has.'"

Another example of honest dialog about racism was when a former human resources recruiting and hiring professional and I had an honest conversation about how referring clients or candidates for hire in certain companies or departments would go down. Some departments preferred that the candidates we referred for hire, be a non-minority. They did this as late as the 1990s! I replied to one client, "I hope the phone isn't bugged—you know I need to present *all* qualified candidates." After the call, my boss said, "That may be so, but you will be wasting your time." In this year of 2020, I would have done better. I would have worked harder to find the best minority candidate to prove Martin Luther King Jr.'s call to action; that we judge on the content of character, not the color of skin.

These dialogs shed light. They may be little things, but done with the right attitude, they are not small things. Indeed this kind of honest discourse provides a necessary and continuing education for all of us, including those in a job or career who feel intimidated to look the other way.

It is each of us who will find the courage to stay awake and assist in the myriad of ways to rid our world of this systemic racist sickness. It is each of us who will determine the level of support we can give one another in a pandemic.

Beyond a collective call to action, is doing the inner awareness and shadow work that I am passionate about. Within the paradigm of the Enneagram is the potential for a transformation from the habitual personality with all of its challenging patterns, to claiming your unique strengths and knowing your essence at a deep level. I have been a missionary for deepened consciousness for close to twenty years, and it is work that pays big dividends in our emotional wellness, which, of course, contributes to our physical state.

Another question for reflection is, what are some of the proactive ways we can gain acceptance of our shadow and light and deepen compassion for others? We can be sure that doing our inner work where we name issues and habits and things that no longer serve us, and claim our gifts and unique aspect of spirit, not only raises our level of well-being and health, but also raises the vibration for all connected to us. Indeed this kind of deepened consciousness can ripple out father than we could ever see.

In my book, *Who You Are Meant To Be: The Enneagram Effect* (Transcendent Publishing, 2019), I speak about this inner work of personal higher consciousness, which the time-honored Enneagram offers so many across the globe.

I'll close with a piece on imagining a different world that I hope will move you to continue to stay awake, even when it is hard to do so, to choose higher consciousness for yourself, and insist upon it in the leaders you vote for, because it is another not-so-small thing that we can all do.

Imagine a world with more self-awareness, where people (where leaders of all countries), become aware of their area of avoidance—of what issues they were in denial around. Imagine the freedom of standing in our truth and not projecting our shadow aspects onto others.

Imagine a world where people do not run on autopilot with their emotional passions but are aware of their underlying programs or driving energies, such as correctional anger, pride, over-identification with roles and image, envy, avarice/withholding, fear and doubt, distraction, over-control, and self-forgetting or over-dialing down to please others.

Imagine being committed to self-awareness about your particular automatic responses, in the same moment that emotion/emotional passion gets triggered. This means leaning into it, naming it, handling it, and finally managing it and not the other way around.

Imagine a world of people who are intentional about having good emotional health and who can see clearly how this clarity may affect their physical health.

Think about the consequences of a conscious world for couples, friends, families, companies, and even countries. The potential for our greatness within this inner work is staggering.

Stress is a reality in life, but with the Enneagram inner work, it is about making it less of a reality in our lives."

We know our individual and the collective's stresses of 2020 with the health crisis called Covid-19. We are experiencing the movement for all lives to matter—black and brown people, or any minorities, including women, the LGBTQ community, the elderly, and the impoverished.

As stressful as the movement toward more fairness may be, we hear this deeper call to stop discrimination against all minority groups and feel a healing and new growth. We also hear a call to heal the divide within ourselves.

What is certain to me is that doing inner work, be it in therapy (healing) or your choice of a learning tool that deepens higher consciousness within, the stresses in our life will be easier to bear and work through. It is our nature to feel peace, and like with everything we value, being aware and awake contribute to that peace.

Chapter *Nine*

Unwrapping Your Authenticity

By Carmen Jelly Weiss

Carmen Jelly Weiss

Carmen Jelly Weiss is a registered psychotherapist, clinical supervisor, and best-selling author. Carmen's journey as a counselor and psychotherapist began in 1989 with a degree in psychology and sociology. She also holds a Master's degree in counseling psychology. Carmen specializes in holistic psychotherapy for the treatment of trauma, addictions, depression, anxiety, grief, and life transitions.

Carmen's approach is somatically-based and attachment-oriented. She integrates psycho-dynamic and dialectical behavior therapy (DBT), internal family systems (IFS), compassionate inquiry, and mindfulness. Carmen is the owner and creator of her private practice, New Perceptions, in North Bay, Ontario. She also provides online telehealth video sessions so people can connect from the comfort of their homes. She is passionate about empowering people to rediscover their authentic selves, and encourages people to access their self-compassion and worthiness to live their lives wholeheartedly and courageously.

In collaboration with Natalie Lebel and Suzanne Rochon, Imagine New Perceptions on Being Human was founded. Together, they boldly create WER3 podcasts connecting concepts, ideas, and insights. They manifested the Raw Risky & Real framework, which leads them into the frontiers of healing, counseling, empowerment, and spirituality. Their desire is to help people achieve their goals and manifest the lives they deserve. You can follow WER3 on Podbean, iTunes, Spotify, and Facebook.

Carmen enjoys deep laughter, running, and yoga. Her most cherished pastime is spending time with her family. She is beyond grateful for her husband Tony, twin daughters Taylor and Loren, and her youngest daughter, Sydney. She is also blessed with a son-in-law, Zach, and has been gifted with two precious grandsons, Milo and Emry.

For more information, or to connect with Carmen, you can explore her website at www.newperceptions.ca or email at carmen.jelly@newperceptions.ca.

Unwrapping Your Authenticity
By Carmen Jelly Weiss

"Your conflicts, all the difficult things, the problematic situations in your life are not chance or haphazard. They are actually yours. They are specifically yours, designed specifically for you by a part of you that loves you more than anything else. The part of you that loves you more than anything else has created roadblocks to lead you to yourself. You are not going in the right direction unless there is something pricking you in the side, telling you, "Look here! This way!" That part of you loves you so much that it doesn't want you to lose the chance. It will go to extreme measures to wake you up, it will make you suffer greatly if you don't listen. What else can it do? That is its purpose." ~ A.H. Almaas

This quote gives me goosebumps, shakes, and rattles my soul. It compels me to abruptly stop and take a deep breath. The fires burning around me fade. When I get caught up in confusion or an ego tornado, that part of me whispers softly, and I listen. That wasn't always my story. Rarely did I listen to my inner knowing; thus, I have suffered greatly. Every painful fire and tornado experience has become an important life lesson. I can look at my pain as a problem to be rid of, or I can ask myself where this is leading me.

Authenticity versus Attachment

Perhaps that place inside you, that part of you, nudged you to buy this book. Perhaps it is the magical force of your authentic self. As stated in the quote above, we all have that part of us that loves us more than anything else. I imagine this part as our essence, which glows with a magnificent, radiant white light. As we grow and age, essence develops, and it is faced with a double challenge: it must learn to function in a chaotic world, while also remaining connected to us.

We slowly become alienated from our essence through the development of perception and behavior known as the personality or ego. Our essence is tucked away and lost to our coping strategies. The journey back to our authentic self requires a courageous heart. The courage to heal is an ongoing journey whereby we come to terms with our past while moving bravely forward into the future.

Psychiatrist Alice Miller writes, "The truth about our childhood is stored up in our body, and although we can repress it, we can never alter it. Our intellect can be deceived, our feeling manipulated, our perceptions confused, and our body tricked with medication. But someday the body will present its bill, for it is as incorruptible as a child who, still whole in spirit, will accept no compromises or excuses, and it will not stop tormenting us until we stop evading the truth." The truth will keep nudging us until we find our way back. In the meantime, we disconnect from our essence because we block painful experiences. Maya Angelou writes in the opening lines of *I Know Why the Caged Bird Sings,* "I hadn't so much forgot as I couldn't bring myself to remember."

Dr. Gabor Maté, and attachment research, suggest that we have two basic needs: attachment and authenticity. Whenever there is a conflict between the two basic needs, we must choose attachment for survival. We choose attachment over authenticity because we are hard-wired for connection and belonging. Personality parts are created so we can survive in our families of origin. I suffered greatly when I didn't listen to my authentic self pricking me in the side and telling me, "wrong way," "not now," or "this relationship is toxic." Rather than listening to my authentic self, my adaptive strategies were running my life. Our brilliant minds create stories that protect us from recalling painful experiences, while at the same time keeping us connected and attached.

Digging Deeper: Going Inside To Identify Parts

Are you ready to dig a little deeper? Have you ever noticed that there isn't only one of you? I do not mean that in a "you're crazy" kind of way. I'm not talking dissociative identity disorder or multiple personalities. Simply, it means that there isn't only one version of us. Richard Schwartz, the founder of Internal Family Systems (IFS), posits that once parts make space, we can all have access to the core of who we are, the "essence." IFS is a cutting-edge form of psychotherapy that has been spreading rapidly since 2000. This approach assumes each individual possesses a variety of sub-personalities, or "parts," and attempts to get to know each of these parts better to achieve healing. We are often in a struggle with various parts of ourselves, and that creates confusion. It's a painful and difficult dance. All the while, our authentic self is nudging us to look inside.

A courageous heart listens to this inside voice. Brené Brown states: "Speaking honestly and openly about who we are, about what we're feeling, and about our experiences (good and bad) is the definition of courage." Do you have the courage to listen to the voice that is nudging you? Richard Schwartz dubbed this voice, or non-part, as "the self." Instead of resisting pain and discomfort, I invite you to consider consciously exploring your parts. I invite you to step beyond reactive behavior.

When we stop resisting, the resurrection of our authenticity becomes possible. Yes, the part that is nudging becomes seen and heard. It takes time, and ongoing practice, but the new dance is graceful and powerful. With a courageous heart, we can move from wounds to wellness. Inside each of us is a part that was hurt, betrayed, or abandoned. It is important to create a compassionate, loving relationship with the child you once were. Be intentional about getting to know all parts: a baby, a perfectionist, a people pleaser, an overachiever, an inner critic, and many more.

You might feel split, caught in a real schism, when fires are burning all around you or there are storms that never seem to stop. Dr. Gabor Maté states, "Where there is tension, bring attention." With compassionate self-inquiry, you can get curious about body sensations, emotions, and parts, which are often in conflict with each other. Each of us can communicate with the parts that hold and protect our wounds. With meditation, visualization, and mindfulness, you can enter this safe space. Space is created with courage, curiosity, compassion, and non-judgment.

Let's look at a part which most of us have, commonly known as the inner critic. We might have had harsh or critical parents, teachers, coaches, or bosses, so it is not surprising we judge ourselves. When you feel down, blue, or defeated, what story do you create in your mind? Are you tender-hearted and self-compassionate, or do you feel a big thumbs down? For most people, the inner critic part is louder than the self-nurturer part. Check in with yourself and see if these parts are in balance. Our inner critic holds a positive intent for us but sometimes takes on an extreme role. It can become less destructive and more cooperative once its concerns are addressed.

The Deep Dive: Exploring Polarity and Loving All Parts

Are you ready to dive deeper? In a quiet, still, place, think about a recent difficult experience. You will discover two or more parts of yourself in conflict. I experienced this polarization when considering writing for this book. Part of me knows that I can allow wisdom to flow through me, and then this other part is screaming, "No, no, don't be seen!" I have parts of me that are excited to write and share my insights. I also have parts of me that are paralyzed with fear. My perfectionist part and my people-pleasing parts are concerned and trying to protect me from judgment and shame. When I am connected to my essence, I invite these parts into a conversation, and I find out why they are trying to protect me.

Mirror, mirror on the wall who is the fairest of them all? Who do you see in the mirror? Do you see your inner critic or another part? Twenty-nine years ago, I wore the perfect shade of pink lipstick on the delivery table at 5:00 a.m. when I gave birth to my twins. I now realize my perfectionist part was desperately attempting to find peace in a terrifying early birth experience. When I look at confidant and radiant people, the thread that seems to link them together is that they dare to love all parts of themselves. On a good day, I feel a sense of vibrating energy running through my body. When I am not having a good day, another part is present. It could be my inner critic, people pleaser or perfectionist parts who all hold an old core belief—I am not enough.

Our parts often carry strong emotions such as anger, fear, disgust, and sadness. They are parts that carry burdens from our past. These parts are hiding and protecting our raw wounds. The parts are little children stuck in terrible roles. Until we heal from the hurt, we will always need our protective parts. We need to reparent these parts with compassion. Most parts are quite young when they come online and are forced into a role for survival or attachment. In this present moment, they believe you are perhaps five or six years old. You can experiment by focusing on a part, perhaps your inner critic, and ask how old it is. Most people will get a single digit when they ask this question.

For some people, trauma causes the development of complex parts that are so strong, they think they are these parts. You are *not* these parts. Dr. Gabor Maté explains that trauma is not the event that happens to us, but rather what occurs inside our bodies. It is a disconnect from our authentic self. This pain gets frozen in time and thinks it still has to hide. Think of a time that you felt humiliated or shamed in your life. I recall being teased because I had a face full of freckles. My passion for make-up was birthed so that I could hide my freckles, my shame. What did you do? Most people want to leave this painful experience behind. The impulse is to lock them away, so other parts carry all the feelings and burdens. We usually are not aware that we are hiding all these sensitive hurt and shamed parts. There is an energy that is making sure the pain doesn't get touched. "There is no agony like bearing an untold story inside you." ~ Zora Neale Hurston

Before our painful experiences, our authentic self played the lead role. The protective parts took over. We try to move on without our authenticity, and we lose access to our natural gifts. We have to go to those protectors, the various parts, and have conversations. To do this, you have to be in a calm and curious mindful state.

Find a Target Part and Get Curious

In a mindful state, I can focus on any part, for example, my competitive part. I notice her presence when I don't appreciate a nice beautiful run in nature because I am too concerned about my pace or my race time. I may also notice other parts present, such as my anger, so I ask that part to step aside. I kindly request for the part that is angry to give me some space so I can get curious about my competitive part. Once the anger steps aside, I engage my competitive part and discover that she had to work hard to be seen and successful. My part wants me to understand that there is pain underneath. She tells me about a time when she wished she was a better figure skater but didn't have the confidence to shine. I can then go into that time and be with that child part. She was always picked last to be on a team sport. She is small and appreciates having me there.

I ask her if there is anything she wants me to do. She would like me to hold her and to feel safe and special. I ask her if she is ready to leave that time and place and come with me. She is afraid because the world is not safe, and she might not fit in. She is open to going to a safe place. In my mind's eye, I show her a nice beach with sand and water. I tell her that she never has to go back to the painful time and that I am taking care of her now. I check to see if she can let go and unload the feelings. The water feels healing, and we take the pain into the ocean. I then bring in the competitive part with her stopwatch and marathon schedule, and she is willing to give us her timer and consider a new role. She is done with control and much more relaxed. Her new role is that of a kind cheerleader. When running, my authentic self can now appreciate the beautiful rolling hills, birds chirping, colorful flowers, and magnificent trees.

I invite you to engage in this exercise with curiosity and kindness. Once we get to know our parts, they feel understood, and this creates a big magical shift. When the part is witnessed and seen, transformation happens. This practice works with all psychological problems because we do not judge behavior. This brings an understanding of our pain and challenges. The authentic self is the place we access all our parts. This compassionate, calm, and connected self is in everybody. When we access self, we will automatically start to change and heal.

We see other people shining and glowing. It's like they swallowed the full moon. Some of us shrink and don't take up much space. We are frightened to be real, so we create parts to hide our gifts. Unwrap your authenticity. Welcome and love all your parts: the people pleaser, the perfectionist, the overachiever, and the addict. If you could be the person of your dreams, who would you be? Our challenge is to get to know all our parts, so they can unburden and allow our authenticity to shine. With a courageous healing heart, I invite you to unwrap your gift and step into your real authentic power.

"Sometimes being real means allowing pain or accepting a painful truth. Yet something in us aligns with an inner ground of authenticity when we are real. We love it because of its inherent rightness in our soul, the sense of 'Aha, here I am, and there is nothing to do but be.'"

~ A.H. Almaas

Chapter

Ten

Curious Courageous Truth: The Journey from Racism to Equity

By Donna Kiel

Donna Kiel

Donna Kiel is a thought leader, an inspiration ignitor, a change-maker, and a haven for those seeking their truth. Donna's unique ability to inspire others to discover and realize their highest and truest potential has provided countless women and men the insights and tools to live lives of purpose, meaning, and success. Donna combines her thirty-plus years of success as a counselor, leader, and teacher with her distinctive ability to inspire those she meets with her ability to see in others that which they often are yet to see. Donna's experiences, training, and her engaging and welcoming style provide others the compassion and connection needed to discover their individual genius and passion. Donna is a coach, mentor, best-selling author, professor, and architect of change who works for equity and empathy in every context. Donna holds a doctorate in educational leadership and is a certified counselor and trained life coach. Donna created the 3E program with practical tools of empathy, equity, and equanimity, which lead organizations and individuals to experience success. Donna is often sought for innovative change efforts by organizations and individuals seeking solutions to systemic and life challenges. Donna inspires, enlivens, and creates useful and practical solutions. Donna is the epitome of inspiration and integrity for those seeking meaning, insight, and concrete answers to the next steps in life. Donna is currently a professor, speaker, coach, and mentor offering workshops, individual coaching, and life mapping sessions. She can be reached at drdonnakiel@gmail.com or through her website at https://donnakiel.com.

Curious Courageous Truth: The Journey from Racism to Equity
By Donna Kiel

I stood in front of the mirror, looking intently into my eyes. My hands shook as I read the words on the index card, "I am safe and trusting." I had a stack of cards with words and phrases assuring my safety, success, and belonging. Affirmation cards are another strategy to ease anxiety and spark courage. Rituals like saying affirmations are attempts to get me through the stories of doom and the cowardice I create in the wild, untamed world of my mind. I've long believed courage was what other people had and what I had was a combination of luck and the keen ability to fake my way through life, as I live with a bundle of fears so numerous they are in charge of me. I fear I will disappoint someone, anger my boss, get in trouble, lose something, fart at the wrong time, say something stupid, not say something, get lost, or the biggest fear that my life will end without me having made a difference.

Rather than grow in courage, I have grown in skill at covering up the tsunami of fear that greets me the moment I wake up. I masterfully wear a costume of a calm, peaceful woman who confidently moves through life speaking eloquently about self-awareness and ease. I truly should get an Oscar for the best actress in the role of a woman who is peaceful and productive. Pretending has served me well. I can smile and say yes with glee, when on the inside I am screaming, "Help me!"

I have tried everything to strengthen my courage muscle, from therapy to coaching and reading volumes of psychology and self-help books. I even earned advanced educational degrees with the belief that the more initials after my name, the more courageous I would become. Instead, I became a stressed out and anxious mess with lots of initials after my name.

I have pushed away from the fears by becoming a workaholic and master people pleaser. I'm the one who attends to all the details rather than engages with people in the work. Working endless hours with a task list that is never-ending has been the greatest distraction to my fear of inadequacy. If I could work harder, longer, do more, give more, then perhaps I would finally feel worthy. Rather than worthy, the only thing I felt was exhausted and desperate. I dreamed of catching up, of sitting still, of writing that New York Times best-selling book so I could prove my worth. Each day I would promise myself that this was the day I would slow down. Each day as I rushed to get to my endless meetings, I would envision coming home and sitting still without the wave of fear washing over me. I kept thinking that having accomplishment after accomplishment would grow my courage to a level where I could finally become a woman of authenticity and worthiness.

Days, months, and years have passed by, and my workload increases alongside my detachment and longing to belong. Rather than more courageous and authentic, I was worn out, empty, and broken. My heart knew I needed to stop running, doing, and worrying.

I was sitting at my desk when an alert came to my phone saying Illinois is in a stay at home order. The novel coronavirus transported me to a new ocean of emotion. I saw people around me going into a fearful panic. I listened to colleagues and family grow upset at the thought of working from home. Not me. I felt a wave of joy and relief. The stay at home order was my dream come true. Finally, I could stop racing to be the people-pleasing "doer" of everything that everyone wanted. I was elated. Finally, I could be still, and perhaps for the first time, I could find the *me* I kept searching for.

The wave of happiness lasted all of a day. As daily briefings of deaths, job losses, and the unknown filled the media, I was filled with a heightened fear that now I could not prove my worthiness with work and production. Who am I without my fancy job title of professor and coach? Who am I without doing for my family or friends?

The stay at home order took away the distractions that kept me from truly knowing me. The pandemic was becoming my awakening to me—the me who allowed fear and insecurity to consume her with busyness and detachment. I wondered if I had somehow visualized the pandemic into being as an instinctual coping mechanism to save my life. I had longed for connection and meaning in my life, and now, without racing around, the universe and God were giving me another chance.

I wish I could say I rose to the occasion, but rather, I quickly pivoted to find a way to be at home and replicate the busy schedule that had consumed me. I became a Zoom master who filled each minute of the day with meetings, new ideas, and making lists to send to my boss to prove I was working. I couldn't sit alone in a room with myself, so I virtually filled the room.

It was during a webinar I created to help parents and teachers cope with the stress of remote teaching that the bottom fell out. As I was teaching my CALM method of centering, awareness, learning, and movement, I fell apart. My voice cracked as I encouraged the participants to reflect in quiet and to disconnect from technology. Tears filled my eyes as I described how self-awareness and self-care must be a priority to show up for others.

I was exhausted, spent, and lost. Sorrow and hopelessness consumed me. I slammed down my laptop screen and screamed, "Stop!" I had to stop. My heart raced, and I couldn't catch my breath. I was panting and crying. My face felt hot, and my chest heavy. I couldn't breathe. My truth was dying.

I went back to that mirror, looked in my eyes, and shouted, "Enough! No more. It is time to stop." My entire body pushed away from the wanting of praise from working hard. My heart ached to be connected to me.

I put away the affirmation index cards and started getting curious. What truly brings me joy? What do I want to do with each day? How do I love me the best way I can? I began a new ritual of checking in with curiosity.

Then it happened. I watched a black man be murdered by a white police officer. My vulnerable heart worn down from the pandemic was now ripped apart by the murder of George Floyd. I feel ashamed that it took this death to shake me. He couldn't breathe. I let my ego convince me I couldn't breathe. How did I become so numb to the systemic racism that has been killing black people for as long as I remember? He couldn't breathe because there was a knee on his neck. I had become someone I didn't know.

My fears of being unworthy or of not meeting the needs of others seem so completely ridiculously insignificant. How dare I waste so much effort and time on petty anxieties of my self-absorbed ego while black people are being silenced and disregarded? How had I missed the evidence of racism that not only surrounds me but to which I contributed?

Shame and sorrow fill every ounce of my being. Hearing George Floyd call to his mama before taking his last breath was that loud call to truth. How could this happen? How could I be a part of a culture that had made no progress in the equity and dignity of all humans? The questions filled my soul alongside the pain. I wanted to learn. I want to listen. I did not want to speak. Each time I heard a white person speak or a white colleague tell their story of inclusion, I became angry. I wanted to scream, "Shut up and listen!"

During the weeks that followed the atrocious murder of George Floyd, I found myself consumed with anger when I would hear or read about white people saying to black people, "You know I love and accept you, and this is not me." I didn't understand my anger at white people saying, "This is not me." Why did I want them to stop talking? Why did I find every story, every social media post, every darn email to be disgusting and useless untrue vitriol? Why did I want to be quiet and to listen?

No longer was I consumed with my self-absorbed worries. Now, I want to face the truth. I want to face the truth of my journey within the dark valley of racism as a white woman. I want to completely shed the image I have of myself as a liberal, accepting, vigilant civic activist because obviously, that hasn't been good enough. I wanted to know who I was and how did I get here.

My experience of racism began in 1968 when I was nine years old. In the fall of 1968, I was standing with my Girl Scout troop friends in downtown Springfield, Illinois, the state's capital. Our field trip from Chicago was an exciting time to see the historical landmarks that were once the home of Abraham Lincoln. As a nine-year-old Girl Scout, I was happy to be with friends and earn another badge for my uniform sash.

I stood looking at the capitol building and the sea of black, brown, and white faces. I was a quiet and introverted child. This day was no different. I stood quietly next to my best friend, Carol, who towered over me. I would watch people and listen. Other kids would often say, "Stop starring," as I studied their outgoing talk in amazement.

This day, like most days, I was watching the people around me. As the young black girl quickly walked toward me, I remember thinking she must need something from our Girl Scout leader. The sting of the slap of her hand across my face left me stunned and in pain. I could feel my face turning red with both embarrassment and throbbing pain. I wanted to cry yet didn't want the attention. My heart was pounding out of my chest. Shame filled my body.

For whatever reason, perhaps a history of shame and feelings of unworthiness, I felt I deserved the slap. I had been staring at the group of black children. The fear, the confusion, and all my feelings were silenced. I was convinced that the anger of the young black woman that motivated her random slap of my face was due to my inadequacy. Somehow, I deserved this.

As a teenager in the 1960s and 1970s, I quietly opposed the Vietnam War. I professed myself as a feminist. As a student in a liberal, all-girl Catholic high school, I convinced myself that being friendly to the one black girl in my classes made me an anti-racist. I attended a university in the city of Chicago that was diverse and again convinced myself because I would be kind to my black fellow students that I was open-minded and inclusive.

In the 1990s, as a high school counselor and administrator, when the school encountered a heinous act of racism, I led efforts to support students in a walkout. I listened to black parents passionately share their hurt and wounding over the racism of our teachers. I convinced myself that what they were describing was not me. I was anti-racist. I knew the pain. I was different. I was wrong. None of those stories of my youth matter. None of those experiences make me an anti-racist. None of those experiences do anything but show my white privilege.

In May of 2020, the murder of George Floyd broke open this country, and it broke me open. After 400 years, we saw the truth, and I wanted *my* truth. As a high school principal, I worked with black and brown students to make sure they graduated and had the same opportunities as white students. I believed I fought racism in my school. I even had connected my daughter with one of our black students to be her friend in college. I believed the racism and systemic violence against black individuals and the white supremacy that was finally being talked about were about them—not me. I was wrong. Again, I confused my cowardice and wanting to keep the peace with being an anti-racist.

Regardless of my work, my values, and my desire to be inclusive, to understand, to fight for equity and access, racism was also mine. How could it not be me? I am white. I cannot be color blind. I do not want to be color blind. I want to love and accept others, but it is impossible until I love and accept myself. Courage is not about the bravery of facing fear. Courage is curiosity and truth. Courage is asking the questions that lead to the truth of who we are and then finding the way to love that person.

The emotional and physical pain I felt that day in 1968 in Springfield was not my badge of honor as I had made myself believe. I cannot know the depth of pain experienced by those who are black in a country that has dismissed black lives in favor of the economic gain and power of white people. Because I won the DNA lottery and was born white, I was also born with white privilege. I need to learn how that privilege has deeply hurt black people. I need to learn more and talk less. I need to feel the shame of making mistakes on the journey of equity and face the truth of the wonderfully messy and imperfectly perfect person I am. If I am to be a solution for equity, and to truly be an ally, I must know and love who I am now and who I can become.

The most courageous thing I have ever done in my life happened after being worn down by a pandemic and broken open by heinous acts of racism. The most courageous thing I have ever done is to look deeply at myself and find what I do not know about me and my own identity as a white woman. Now, I am committed to showing up and speaking up. I now say the uncomfortable truth when with white people—and it is hard. I listen rather than speak with black men and women—and it is hard. I get curious about me, and the truth shows up—and it is hard. Becoming part of the solution means shedding our protective story and stepping courageously into the truth.

Chapter

Eleven

Coaching Past Your Fears to Find Your Courage

By Amy I. King

Amy I. King

Amy I. King is a certified life coach and owner of Your Phenomenal Life, LLC. She taught in public education for a decade before returning to school for her coaching certification. She is a contributing author of international bestsellers: *Inspirations: 101 Uplifting Stories for Daily Happiness*, *Manifestations: True Stories of Bringing the Imagined into Reality*, and *The Grateful Soul: The Art and Practice of Gratitude.*

Amy enjoys spending time with friends, listening to the great music of a variety of genres, reading (of course!), writing, and adventure. She enjoys travel both solo, and with loved-ones, she loves meeting new people and making new connections.

Amy has overcome a plethora of challenges that make her the woman she is today. She was born with Spina Bifida, which requires her to use a wheelchair. Despite the many challenges she has faced, she has created a life that is filled with wonderful people who have helped her create amazing memories. She has most recently overcome breast cancer. Every challenge, Amy believes, is put before us to help us to evolve and grow into the greatest version of ourselves.

Amy's greatest joy is using her personal experiences and wisdom to help others move past their personal blocks and outdated beliefs to becoming empowered to live the life of their dreams. She loves developing relationships with her clients built on trust and vulnerability. She focuses on coaching teens and women. She is currently coaching and working on her first solo book, *Messy Wheels: Stories from Where I Sit*, available on Amazon in 2021. She can be reached at (916) 718-0914. She welcomes the opportunity to work with you to help you build the life of your dreams.

Coaching Past Your Fears to Find Your Courage

By Amy I. King

Courage, they say, cannot exist absent fear. From time to time, we all allow fear to manipulate and keep us from realizing our passions and potential. As a life coach, I have clients who come to me with various challenges or life situations that they need help navigating. The number one stumbling block that clients come across is their fear. I use several techniques to help my clients break through the fears that are holding them back from their phenomenal life.

Clients come to me with fears or blocks that they need to clear out of their way—more than all other issues combined. The client must first identify what they are afraid of or what is blocking them. One of the essential skills of a life coach is active listening. It is imperative to building a trusting relationship that my clients know that I am there for them, no matter what they have to say. Listening to my clients to give them empathy and compassion helps them feel comfortable when opening up to me.

Helping the client look at new ways of thinking about fear is essential. Asking questions such as, "What are you feeling right now? What do you think is blocking you? What can you do about it?" When the client is ready, I will pose a question such as, "What would happen if you—?" Then I present the worst-case scenario that could happen if my client takes the action that they are fearing. The client will typically sit in thought for a few moments. When the worst-case scenario is in front of a client, often, it's implausible to happen even if one has taken action.

Asking questions that will help clarify what is happening to them will move us toward the action steps. Issues such as "What fears or concerns do you have surrounding this goal?" Or, "What might get in the way of this goal?" Both help the client to get focused on the action steps that they will need to enact.

Working with Fears

When one is dealing with fear, the fight or flight response is always in play. Fight or flight increases our cortisol levels, which may result in shallow or rapid breathing. The client must calm down and slow their breathing. Focused breathing, yoga, and meditation work to calm the mind and body. I like to take my clients through a breathing exercise when they are amenable.

Breathing Exercise:

Close your eyes, take a deep cleansing breath in for the count of five.

Hold for a count of five

Release for a count of ten.

Repeat this five times.

Breathing out longer ensures the clearing of all of the negative energy.

Once the client is calm, I ask them what brings them comfort and solace. A smile breaks out, followed by some reminiscence. They typically speak about their children or a place or item. It may be a book that they love or a memory they hold dear to their heart. It is then that I know they are in their center. Once centered, we can get to the real work. Many times, clients are anticipating something that is imminent, such as an important job interview, responsibilities of new parenthood, a new job, or an awkward conversation. They may be trying to break through fear or a pattern they would like to break. In breaking patterns, it's important to note that the client must decide to make the life change required to break whatever pattern may cause them to struggle.

Let's look at a coaching session so that you can see how it works. I will use an actual scenario from one of my client sessions, but I will change my client's name to Lois.

Lois is a middle-aged woman who is trying to find her place in the world post-divorce. She has free time every other weekend while her children are with their father. Throughout their 17-year marriage, Lois has devoted most of her energy to taking care of her now ex-husband and their three children. Lois feels that she has lost her identity as a result. She has fallen into a pattern and desperately wants to get rid of this pattern to create a more fulfilling life.

I asked Lois who she was before she got married. One of the things that Lois immediately starts talking about is her adventures. She tells me about the time she once camped for a week by herself. I asked her to close her eyes and go back to that time and space when she camped alone. When I asked her to describe herself during that time in her life, she said, "I was one of those people who was never afraid of anything. I would go anywhere and do almost anything if I felt like doing it." I asked her to describe herself now. Her response was, "I feel like I am self-sacrificing, unfulfilled, and exhausted to the point of being done." This once brilliant light was burning out like an old lightbulb. She had too much life left in her to simply keep going in her unfulfilling life. We had to do something. So, I took her through an exercise to help in the process of making life changes.

The first thing I did was ask her what life pattern or habit is complicated for her to change? She responded that she didn't know who she was anymore, and she was tired of her life role of serving the needs of others and disregarding herself. I asked her what some of the benefits would be, should she change her patterns. Her voice took an upturn as she said, "Well, I'd love to take a class or two, start dating if I remember how, and maybe make a few new friends, or perhaps take a solo trip, but that sounds scary." Then I asked her how she benefits if this pattern remains. She said, "That means I don't have to go outside of my comfort zone, and I don't have to be vulnerable." I then asked what she would lose by changing this behavior. She said that the only thing she'd lose is her low self-esteem. That's when she had the epiphany and realized that she had to take action. She had allowed herself to lose *her* during her marriage and raising children. Her self-esteem had plummeted. Her sense of self was deeply rooted in what she did for her ex-husband and her children. The final question I asked was, "What does it cost you if you do not make the change?" She said, "It costs me my life." We talked further and came up with a few action steps for her to take. In the following two weeks, she decided that she would create a dating profile and that she was going to join a meetup group. I also assigned her a few exercises that help one narrow down passions. It sometimes amazes me how much progress one can make in a single session. I'm happy to report that she followed through on her action steps and is now creating a new, more fulfilling life. She is figuring out who she is in the process.

After one of the coaching sessions, I realized that I needed to use the skills that I had been attaining from my coaching courses and get busy changing my life. I wasn't complaining. However, I was exhausted, having experienced tremendous loss throughout the past ten years that I had taught school. I had lost one close family member after another, year after year. I was helping others, and it was time to help me rediscover myself.

For the longest time, I had a fear of going anywhere alone. My twenties had been riddled with anxiety about being alone in a public setting. Even going to the grocery store was brutal. Fast forward to a much more independent version of myself. On a recent trip to Maui with a girlfriend, I felt a pull inside. Something was there for me on that island. I needed to find out what or who it was. My friend Shawn, while doing some bodywork on me shortly before my scheduled departure, said, "You're going to meet a man who is surrounded by gold." I thought to myself, "Okay, sounds good to me!"

At first, when I booked my trip, I was scared. I mean, who travels alone in a wheelchair? I even asked several friends if they wanted to meet me over there for a few days. No one was available to go, so I was heading to Maui for ten days, just me, myself, and I. Adventure awaited! As my fear dissipated, it was replaced with anticipation for the adventure that lie before me. I packed what I thought I needed into my large suitcase and packed what I wanted on the plane into my small matching periwinkle carry-on. The shuttle to the airport arrived on time. Having traveled extensively, I was familiar with the driver and his family. We exchanged conversation, as I inquired about his children and grandchildren.

The entire trip to the islands couldn't have gone better. The flights were smooth, getting my luggage was a breeze, and as I rolled down to the rental car shuttle stop, I noticed it was already there waiting for my arrival. The car was also waiting for me, a red Nissan Altima complete with hand controls. I drove down the middle of the island from the airport to my condo. I was all smiles as I drove toward the coast. I had never felt as free as I felt at that moment. I stopped at Safeway for my groceries and headed to the condo. About ten minutes after I arrived, there was a knock at the door. It was a painter asking if he could finish painting a patch on the wall. I felt his energy and let him in. As he painted, we chatted. He was from Virginia, and had moved to Maui to help his uncle in his painting business. He had a cool vibe. We exchanged numbers. He told me if I needed anything, to give him a buzz. I settled in, made some food, and enjoyed the view.

The next day, I did some sightseeing and headed up to a town called Paia. I looked around and came to a store with a deli counter. I was ordering food when a man caught my eye. He was sitting at a small round table with another man. He smiled and said, "Hi." We talked for a while. I learned that he was from California. We exchanged numbers and made plans to hang out that evening. Later, there was a knock at the door. There he was with an enormous smile and a warm hug. We got beers from the fridge and went outside to sit near the ocean. We chatted about our backgrounds, hopes, dreams, and desires. When our hands touched, it was as though we were one energy. Being with him felt like home in an indescribable way. Our souls were definitely vibing. We spent several days together, eating delicious food, exploring new areas, and loving one another. It was as though the Universe said, "I am going to plop you down into one of those incredibly romantic movies—enjoy!"

One day, he came up with the idea that he wanted to take me to a waterfall. I knew that he was well-versed on the island, and he had my trust, so, I complied. We drove to the parking lot leading to the trail toward the waterfalls. I didn't realize he was taking me to a waterfall with a path you had to traverse! I got a little nervous; he wasn't nervous at all. Without grab handles (I push myself, thank you!), he carefully took me down the path, avoiding any pitfalls, as we made progress. Winding down the trail, I could tell he was growing weary. He said it would be worth it when we reached the waterfalls. He was excited to see my reaction.

Finally, we reached the waterfalls. They were majestic. The love that this man, who was a stranger days before, showed me was overwhelming. Tears filled my eyes as I thought of how carefully he moved to get me down those trails. Thankfully, he was watching the waterfall, and not my tears fall. We sat near the water for a while, taking pictures, talking, kissing, and enjoying the surroundings. Then the clouds turned grey. We knew we didn't have much time before they would burst. We made our way back up the hill, which is much more laborious than going down. Midway, it began to pour. Still, he kept going, heaving me through the thickening mud that was grasping at my wheels. People passing asked if they could help, he kept on with a, "Thanks, but we've got it." We made it to the parking lot and sought temporary shelter under the awning crowded with people willing to make space. As the rain let up, we went to the car. My messy wheels caked in mud. He began wiping my wheels with the shirt off his back. "Is there no end to what this man is willing to do?" I thought to myself. We got into the car and drove back. During my ten-day vacation, we spent a great deal of time together.

He showed me the unconditional love I so desperately needed. It was then that I was able to find that unconditional love within myself. He has one of the most tender hearts of any man I have ever had the honor of knowing. He brought me to such a deep love within me. It was a love of a lifetime. Thankfully, the story didn't end there. I write more about our relationship in my book, *Messy Wheels*, due out next year.

I guess I should tell you an essential piece to the story. This man who loved me back to life is named Aurelio. In English, it translates to mean "golden." I had met the man surrounded by gold. He had brought me back to the love within me. For that and him, I am forever grateful! Let go of your fears and hold tight to courage. You never know what you'll discover within yourself.

Chapter
Twelve

A Warrior's Courageous Journey
By Becki Koon

Becki Koon

Becki Koon is a heart-based energy intuitive, Reiki Master, HeartMath coach, life coach, crystal practitioner, and author/speaker. Through her business, Step Stone, Becki empowers people to seek their inner wisdom, while holding space for them to heal, discover, and grow into the next highest version of themselves. She likes to refer to herself as the mid-wife of birthing a person's remembrance of their divine essence or purpose.

Becki's work has recently evolved in a way she never expected. When her husband of 12 years passed, she knew her life was forever changed. What she did not expect was that she would wake up to the ability of communication with him through mediumship. Now, in Reiki and other healing sessions, Becki receives guidance from not only Jack, but her angelic guides and family of light, other people's guides, loved ones who have passed, and ascended masters. The world of channeling higher beings is a gift she says is a salve that has helped her deal with loss and grief. Being in service to others through sharing the process of conscious death has given her an outlet for the compassionate wisdom she gained.

Becki dedicates this story to her love, Jack, and his journey as a spiritual warrior headed into the unknown—his transition from physical form into the mystical realm of the soul. Their process of experiencing conscious death together has changed her life, her work, her very essence, and she vows to continue using the gifts that he so lovingly encouraged her to remember and offer to the world. The transition from physical body to soul essence need not be frightening, but can be a beautiful honoring and celebration of life and love never-ending.

Contact:
stepstone2you@gmail.com
www.beckikoon.com
www.facebook.com/becki.koon.consulting

A Warrior's Courageous Journey
By Becki Koon

Today is significant for me. We, as humans, are so attached to time in this reality, often referred to as the *Third Dimensional Matrix*. Six months ago, at the age of 64, my love left the planet after twelve beautiful years together. I am one of the fortunate. I was blessed to be able to say goodbye and to hold him in my arms. At the same time, I felt the last breath leave his body, no breath to follow, simply complete stillness, a quiet, heart-wrenching peace filling the space that was his alive body only seconds before.

And so ended our twenty-day vigil.

September 4, 2019

How do I begin to say goodbye to you, my love? Cancer is a common word we hear every day, often many times in a day. Yet, when you hear that word in an emergency room from the attending physician, somehow the name takes on a different and surreal meaning. I know as they wheel you away for the CT scan that your life and mine will be forever changed. Somehow, I know the answer to come, and yet, I smile at you and brightly say, "See you in a few minutes, my love."

You get back into the ER, and we joke amidst the smell of sterilizers and the beeping of monitors. Those few minutes seem to drag, and time morphs into a slow dance. "I love you, maybe they will give you a prescription that will help your pneumonia," I say in encouragement.

The doctor enters slowly and sits down. I lovingly look at you as you smile and ask her, "What's the good news?" Her eyes drop, she shakes her head and says, "It's not good news. A nine-centimeter cancerous tumor has taken residence in the right lung, and the cancer has metastasized into the liver, kidneys, lymph nodes, and probably many other organs." I look at you, feeling stunned, full of dread mixed with compassion, but not surprised. You look at me as you say to the doctor, "Well, that must be why I have been feeling bad and coughing up blood. Makes sense." You then look over to the doctor and ask her what the prognosis for time is. "A few days?" you joke and smile.

She looks you squarely in the eyes while fighting back her tears and says solemnly, "Perhaps a couple of months."

Wow! My heart skips, then beats rapidly. My skin immediately flushes, my cheeks burning. Okay then, choices. She says, "You can stay here in the hospital and run through a battery of tests to determine the exact type of cancer and what other organs are affected, and speak to oncology. Treatment might buy you another couple of months, but ask yourself what your quality of life would be. No one can say." She leaves us so we can digest all that we had heard.

I look at you with love; we stare into each other's eyes for a long heartfelt moment, time standing still, and finally, you say, "I am going home. You with me on this, my love?"

With my heart breaking open, feeling exposed and raw, I say, "Of course I am!"

We go home with medications for coughing and pain to help ease your high level of discomfort.

September 13, 2019

You gaze into my eyes, and I can sense what is coming. I don't want to hear it. You lovingly say to me, "You know, my love, this is not about my survival, this is about my passing. This is my path. This is what we both came here to do. You know this. This, too, is part of our journey together, my transition out of this form. You know this is part of your journey going forward, the work you are here to do in the world. You know this, don't you? You are aware that there is no other way for you to gain the wisdom and compassion you will carry in helping others, right?"

I nod my head, yes, I cannot speak, tears flowing down my cheeks, my throat choked off with quiet sobs. And yet, at the deepest part of my being, I know. I do know this to be true—death was intended to be a part of our journey, part of why we came together to experience this side of the power of unconditional love.

You say to me, "My love, I don't want to leave you, but this is what is happening, and I am asking you to help me pass. I want to do this in the most peaceful, conscious, and spiritual way possible. I do not want this to drag on; my body is weak, and I need your help. Will you do this with me?"

I look at you in complete surrender to what is taking place. With all the love, gratitude, and courage I am capable of feeling, I say, "Of course I will be here with you every step of the way, every precious moment, every second. I will not leave your side! I am your wingman, remember?" I smile at you through eyes glazed with tears.

The rest of the night, we hold each other. Every time you get emotional, the breathing spasms start, so we stay calm and in a state of undying love while we hold each other close. We wonder if we will be able to stay connected after your death. Will we be able to continue our relationship from a whole different reality, knowing our soul connection is more than only this life expression?

September 24, 2019

My love, in this transition from physical form to spirit, you will find freedom, an energy that has always meant a great deal to you—freedom from your pain and suffering, from the density of this earthly body, from this matrix. The divine is an energy I wish for you, one with which you are so connected. Please set your spirit free. I can't imagine feeling any greater love in this precious life than I do for you at this moment, and yet, I set you free.

As I say these words, I know it is time to prepare the altar for you that will hold sacred items: rocks, crystals, the Warrior's Prayer, your jewelry, guitar picks, a candle, your favorite oils, all going onto your altar for the honor of passage, a celebration into the next expression.

I play the song that has meant a great deal to you. I often watched you listen, totally absorbed by the music, tears running down your cheeks as your tender heart was taken away by the sheer power of love, beautiful music, and the incredible message shared. My tears are flowing, and I sing along the best I can in tribute to you, a melody of your very essence. The song finishes, and your breath shifts. Your eyes open. I look at Mom and say, "Oh my gosh, I think he is going!"

I rush over to your side, my love, and caress you, caress your face, tell you how much I love you and encourage you to go with your family of light, those present to help you. You gaze up past me, toward the sky as I caress you, crying, placing my hand on your heart as it beats its last beat. Your breath stops, and all is still. Your physical form is done. I hold you and sob tears of sorrow for my profound, agonizing loss, and yet, feeling relief for your freedom from suffering. You made it, my love, you are free! And you made it happen quietly, peacefully, no gasping or struggle, just sleep, the way you hoped it would be, the way your silent spiritual warrior wanted.

I find myself humbled by the awe-inspiring life-force we have while here in our physical bodies. I had no idea how much courage I had within until I witnessed it. I had no idea of the depths love can go until I experienced it. I had no idea of the vastness of the human heart until I lived it.

Now, I feel compelled to share the journey of awareness, of conscious death, with others. We are all human! We all have a soul residing in these physical forms. We all experience emotions, thoughts, and beliefs. We all breathe—breath being the tangible and visible difference between life here and no life here. Death of the physical does not mean the end of the soul.

My love no longer has life here, but I have seen him, I have spoken with him, I am receiving messages from him. The deep spiritual connection we shared has not disappeared; it has transformed, taken on a new life, a new identity, that of eternal, undying love. Does that mean I am not experiencing grief and sadness? Not at all! I find myself in moments that catch my breath, stop me in my tracks, tears always ready to erupt and fall. And yet, I celebrate that I behold him in his soul expression, layered with so much love, light, and bliss that I find myself having no fear of joining him. Many times, I am confused about how I can go on knowing the evidence of his soul energy and wanting to be there with him, but it is not yet time.

It is incredible what the human spirit can do when called to respond in the face of an emergency, in moments of life and death occurrence. We know and experience a courageous heart, actions taking on a life guided by an unseen force within that knows no limits. The thinking-brain gets pushed aside while the divine heart-brain reigns, and the gut-brain responds. As hard as it may be to comprehend, we knew before he passed that this was the journey we chose, that my service in the world would take on a depth and meaning that could not have happened any other way. Jack knew that. He told me to feel into that awareness, to accept the wisdom and strength that would inevitably follow his leaving this planet encompassing my journey of his passing.

What I know—physical death is not the end. It is a passing from one form onto the next, and our loved ones are always near. If we choose to become aware, they could connect. Jack is in constant communication with me now, and I am learning to let go, allow, and trust in this new form of relationship with him. The veil between our dimensions is transparent.

Jack first came to me three weeks after he passed while I was in meditation. I was in a state of open awareness but with no expectations and no thought of him, simply relaxing my mind, spirit, and body. After a few solitary minutes, I noticed someone walking towards me from a bright mist over a strikingly beautiful golden ocean, brilliant, soothing energy surrounding both of us as the form neared. When I realized it was Jack, I felt an energy rush through my body. He was elated, an image of complete joy. He scooped me up in his arms, swinging me around, smiling and laughing. I heard him say, "Hi, my love. Thank you for connecting with me, for making an effort to meet me here in this field of awareness, this frequency." He encouraged me to keep this form of communication going, reminding me that I have the ability; I could meet him here anytime while I build up my intuitive skills for the journey ahead.

When I came out of meditation, I had an internal peace that I had not felt since he had started showing signs of illness. What did I experience? Was it wishful thinking? Was I going crazy?

These random thoughts began to flood my thinking mind. Then I remembered to breathe, taking a breath into my heart, grounding gratitude into my body, and then I knew. I knew he was showing me the soul connection we talked about and that we felt was possible. I have had many more encounters in the months following that continue to validate the channel opening between us, like the radio dial finding the sweet spot for clear reception. I continue to become familiar with his energy field, sense when he is near, listen for his messages. I am walking into untrodden territory. I have always been in awe of people who have the gift of "sight," those who tap into realms of multidimensional reality. Never did I suspect that I would be saying to anyone that I was talking to the spirit of my love who died. I am finding myself in vulnerability as much as I am excited to explore. It takes courage to step into a completely new reality, to share with other people aspects of life that are not easily explained and often judged.

The real test came when I was giving a Reiki session to a client. I had not seen this man since before Jack passed. I did not realize that his daughter had passed away only a week after Jack. When he came into the healing studio, we shared some lovely moments of understanding, of heartfelt love connection through loss.

The session began as always: I focus and allow while the healing Reiki energy flows where it serves the person for their highest need and purpose. I was used to feeling Jack in session with me, often aware of his support, but always something I held close, and did not verbalize. All of a sudden, I heard a female voice speaking, faint, but clearly not Jack. I was wondering what to do, nervous to say anything to my client. But, at her continued insistence, I shared what she was asking me to share with her father. Tears of joy erupted out of him. It was precisely what he needed to hear, and he then shared with me that he had known she would make contact with me; he had just felt it. My lesson was one of trust.

We have inside of us this enormous capacity for evolution, growth, and resiliency to change, no matter how uncomfortable the circumstance. It is when we bypass the thinking-brain and move into our heart-brain that we find the courage to take a chance, to expand into a state of being previously unknown to us. We find we are held with a pearl of divine wisdom that radiates a secure blanket of comfort as we navigate the next step and the next step and the next step.

We are souls living in this remarkable form that falls down and gets back up, that experiences heartbreak and loves again, that feels paralyzed by fear and finds a way to move forward, or break through anyway. Thank you, Jack, for guiding me into my courageous heart.

Chapter

Thirteen

A Stroke of Courage

By Dr. Cheralyn Leeby

Dr. Cheralyn Leeby

I believe we are all heroes of divine descent with courageous hearts. Our wounds for healing and our battlegrounds may differ, but our core strength is universally unearthed when we access our inner drive, determination, focus, and faith. Seeing ourselves push past any defined limitation and struggle, to access our glory, is one of life's most precious presents.

We can, we will, we do! My mother proved that.

I am honored to recognize my mother in this chapter and her ongoing, brave journey with daily strokes of courage. As you might guess, I appreciate all difficulties as gifts for growth.

At this moment, I am finding the courage to "walk that talk." I have a new opportunity to greet life with grace and acceptance as I embrace all that has unfolded over the past week (and months) with the Covid-19 pandemic and the stirring aftermath.

My heart is grieving the unexpected passing of my younger brother last week. Mark was only 49, and he joins our brother, Matthew, in heaven. I dedicate my work in writing and therapy to my sweet siblings,

Matthew Charles (9/2/1969–1/16/1988)

Mark Lewis (11/8/1970-6/20/2020

It was challenging to submit this piece while feeling such sorrow. However, today, more than ever, I am committed to my mission to "feed hope" to myself, my loved ones, and anyone I might inspire towards hope and healing.

Dr. Leeby is a holistic psychotherapist who sees her clients as heroic "healers of self." She is an accomplished writer, speaker, retreat leader, teacher, trauma specialist, art, play, and licensed family therapist. She created Soul Life, LLC, as a platform for community prevention and wellness education. Dr. Leeby's life mission is to "feed hope" to individuals, couples, and families. You can contact her at www.soullife.us.

Stroke of Courage
By Dr. Cheralyn Leeby

10:15 a.m. Christmas morning, 2015

I hold my breath as we speed past the Christmas morning traffic. I wonder if these people are heading to their grandmother's house—over the river and through the woods? I silently pray "Hail Marys" repeatedly. On a rip-roaring, red-siren sleigh ride, we seem to magically appear at the back door of the hospital. I hug Mom for the first time that day, noticing her pale skin against her rosy red sweater. They whisk her away, disappearing through electric doors.

A nurse points me in the direction of a stark, private waiting room. The room designated for life and death conversations. I label it the newsroom. "Is it most often reserved for fatal news?" I wonder. This small, dimly lit space, absent of TVs and magazines, holds the palpable energy of family love and fear. As I sit to collect my thoughts, I remember everything we left at home in a mad dash—the scavenger hunt, warm ovens, twinkling lights, Mom's dog, Gracie. I try to convince myself that Mom will be okay and, soon enough, we'll be at our table enjoying our Christmas dinner together.

It has to be okay.

Most Christmases, our family of four would frantically pack up our presents and parkas and board a plane headed for Utah to spend the holidays with my husband's parents. It was a stressful, squabble-filled time for us to leave town with recitals, exams, and work, but we would feel such relief once on the plane. We looked forward to this yearly opportunity to ski, relax, and sip hot chocolate by the fire with my in-laws.

This particular year, however, we decided to spend our vacation at home in Florida. My husband, Doug, and I were excited to have our 19-year-old son, Chase, home from college, and our 15-year-old daughter, Payton, together again under the same roof. While our other relatives resided out of state, my mother lived less than two miles from us. After her husband passed away, Mom moved to our town to be closer to her youngest grandchildren.

Mom, a lively *Doris Day meets Grace Kelly*, was a former dance teacher who carried her five-foot-two-inch petite frame through life with elegant poise and a light-hearted grace. Mom never liked to sit—she was always on the go. When I was young, she had a dancing school in our garage and later came to love golf, gardening, cooking, and entertaining. Mom had walks, dates, and matches of some sort on her calendar most days of the week. Doug always said she was like catnip, with a steady circle of male admirers attracted to her sunny disposition.

When I told Mom we were staying in town for the holidays, she excitedly invited us to a Christmas Eve service she attended with friends when we were away. We accepted the invitation to try something new.

We dressed in our Sunday best and sat with Mom in the second row. Mom smiled and greeted all the regulars who came over with hugs and merry wishes. She proudly introduced us, easily recalling each of her friends' names, courtesy of a Dale Carnegie course in her 20's. As I watched her, I was inspired to improve my name recollection skills.

The sermon was moving, and I remember thinking, "I see why Mom loves this service." In closing, the congregation sang Christmas carols. Mom belted out each and every word from Jingle Bells to Silent Night—loud and clear. She sang with a slight southern twang even though she grew up in Massachusetts. I nudged Doug's foot, and we glanced at each other, loving her adorable enthusiasm with the songs.

"Silent night, holy night. All is calm, all is bright, sleep in heavenly peace."

Following the chapel service, we had dinner at our favorite Italian restaurant. An energizing chill filled the air, which we warmed with our wine. Mom and I both ordered chicken piccata. We decided to splurge and forget about cholesterol, calories, and meat abstinence. The lemon butter sauce was tangy, salty, and savory. We toasted the year, shared memories, and took family photos standing together outside.

After dinner, Payton and Mom formed a plan to meet at 9:00 a.m. at our house to commence our Christmas festivities. I would make our traditional New England meat pie for breakfast, and an early turkey dinner would follow around 4:00 p.m. Our Christmas dinner replicates Thanksgiving, our favorite meal. Mom agreed to bring her homemade stuffing, gravy, and green bean casserole. I knew Mom would also help me get the turkey cleaned, prepped, and stuffed with apples and herbs, filling our house with the scent of roasted rosemary. I'm one of those squeamish, vegetarian-ish people who dreaded having to touch the turkey carcass, but Mom never seemed to mind.

Before retiring on Christmas Eve, I had some work to do. This year, instead of arranging the kids' presents in piles under the tree, I created a scavenger hunt with limerick clues hidden in each gift. I was proud of my humorous rhymes. I imagined the kids both rolling their eyes but also joyfully racing to decipher each half of the hints they unwrapped. I drifted off to sleep dreaming about this new tradition.

On Christmas morning, I awoke at 6:00 a.m. I gathered my Santa sack of numbered, wrapped riddled gifts, each containing the typed-up clues and headed outside. I planted the presents, two by two, all over the yard, in the mailbox, and behind trees. I was ready for an adventurous day.

As I set the table for our breakfast pie and mimosas, the kids came down in their pajamas, eyeing the base of our decorated tree. They held their words, but I knew they thought that Santa was a little skimpy this year.

I excitedly gave them their morning hugs and kisses. "I have a fun surprise for you!"

Payton exited my embrace as her smile morphed into a furrowed brow, "Where's Mom-Mom?"

I realized it was 9:05—Mom was late. That was a rarity. I called her cell phone—no answer. I waited another ten minutes and tried again, still no answer.

I felt a slow creeping of heaviness, puzzled by her lack of response. I removed our breakfast from the oven and asked Doug if he would drive toward Mom's house to see if there was an accident holding her up. How sad for someone to have a Christmas morning crash. Doug jumped in his car, and Payton joined him for the ride.

Within a few minutes, Doug called me.

"Mom's car is in the garage. I can see it—my garage clicker isn't working. We can't get in. I rang the doorbell, no answer. Payton is going to get on my shoulders and look in the windows."

Mom had white wooden shutters on each window. They could be gently closed on the bottom half but stay open on the top half for the light. Payton hurriedly peered in each window while balancing on Doug's shoulders. The day's treasure hunt became much more serious than I had planned.

Through the master bathroom window, Payton saw a white dog tail move. It was Gracie, Mom's seven-pound Maltipoo. Gracie's presence confirmed it; Mom was in the house. Panic set in.

I raced to find my key to Mom's house, feeling the adrenaline surge through my body. Chase hopped in the passenger seat, and by the time we got there, Doug and Payton were inside. They found Mom curled up on the bathroom floor, with Gracie worriedly keeping watch. Doug called 911. Her words were slurred, and she could not walk.

As I ran in, Doug whispered, "She's not okay."

The paramedics appeared as if they somehow dropped down the chimney, following me to the bedroom. I loved this room, with its clean, crisp linens on a bed that was always perfectly made. Framed family photos and special mementos were carefully placed on her dresser. The room was a bright mix of beachy, French blues and golds—inviting and refined.

The paramedics quickly lifted her onto the rolling metal stretcher. As I ran out the door behind them, I thought to check the oven and stove. They were off. I caught a whiff of the stuffing and green bean casserole waiting in their neatly folded tin-foiled tents.

I ran to the ambulance at the driver's side, "Can I go with her?" I asked in a tear-filled, shaky voice. The driver agreed, but only upfront—and fast. The other paramedic evaluated her in the back. I held in the flood of tears as I hurled myself onto the seat. Reality crept in. The paramedic told me it was most likely a stroke. He assured me that the hospital was ready for her and that they had the best stroke team in our area.

It seemed like only minutes later, we were sitting in the hospital "newsroom." While waiting anxiously for word on Mom, I consulted with "doctor Google" on my phone. Terrified scrolling was intensified by the myriad of information I gathered about strokes.

She actually could die today, and the longer we wait, the greater the chance of death or, at best, some form of permanent paralysis. My heart is pounding. A nurse interrupts my worried wading through the massive sea of possibilities and informs us that Mom will need emergency surgery to stop the stroke. Yup—I just learned that from Wikipedia. I scoot to the edge of my seat.

"Let's do it. Now."

I check my watch. My impatience stirs, and my crossed foot shakes uncontrollably. More test results are needed, and we have to wait on the surgeon, Dr. Miller, who is on his way. Tick tock, tick-tock.

Back to Google, I type furiously. "Who is Dr. Miller?" and "How successful is emergency surgery for a stroke?" Before I can read through enough answers to help my heartbeat slow down, Dr. Miller knocks and enters. This kind and measured man gently shares the gravity of the situation. "She will likely have permanent damage. There is a chance she will not survive the surgery, but I promise to do everything possible."

Tears gush as I try to speak professionally and relay the fact that her veins are small—too small for stents. Memories rush in of this same hospital attempting—unsuccessfully—to surgically insert stents many years ago to open her veins. As a result, Mom committed to reversing her heart disease by following the "eat-nothing-tasty" diet along with a daily exercise program. She followed her doctor's orders with the discipline of an athlete for 20 years, rarely cheating with more than one French fry from her grandchild's plate.

I recall our chicken piccata, and my heart sinks. Was the stroke my fault?

The past struggles I've had with my mother instantly dissolve. I'm not ready to lose her.

"Please hurry," I plead. "Can I see her before surgery?"

I take a deep breath before walking into her room. Smile, say it's going to be ok. Don't cry. Give her hope.

Behind the curtain, I hear the beeps and see the monitors attached to her tiny body. She's awake. I hold her cold, thin hand. "Mom, you have an amazing surgeon. We will be here waiting to see you when it's over. I love you, Mom."

For the next six and a half hours, Dr. Miller would carefully treat the stroke and save her life. If it had not been Christmas Day, with Payton's 9:00 a.m. plan for presents, Mom would have passed away on her bathroom floor. Our Christmas gift was her life.

Mom spent the next several months in and out of hospitals and rehab centers. She never returned to her home, her beautiful blue bedroom, Gracie, or golf. Her new game was a game of patience, acceptance, and will with her body, rather than a ball on the golf course. She courageously pushed through intense physical and emotional pain, and she struggled through therapy even when she could barely open her eyes from the multitude of medications she was prescribed. Mom traded her closet of dancing shoes for sneakers, and her frolic with life was now confined to navigating a wheelchair with one foot.

A year and a half after her stroke, Mom had therapy with a tech who was new to her facility. The woman felt the need to be realistic with Mom, and bluntly told her, "You will never walk again."

No one had said that before. Mom called me immediately after, distressed, and asked if it was true. I said, "Mom, I believe anything is possible."

The Oxford dictionary defines fear as "An unpleasant emotion caused by the belief that someone or something is dangerous, likely to cause harm or a threat." Our beliefs either keep us locked in fear or they hold the key to opening the doors of possibility. For Mom, the fear that she may never walk again inspired a new fight in her.

The next morning, June 15, 2016, Mom left the following message on my phone at 5:05 am.

"Honey, I'm sorry to call so early, but I can move my foot! (crying) It's all pins and needles, but I can move it! I'm sitting in the wheelchair now. I can kick it! (more crying) Call me back. I knocked over Mary. We had to pick her up. Okay, call me."

I envisioned some older crony named Mary, barreled over by Mom's new mobility. I called Mom immediately. "Who's Mary?" I asked. "Is she okay?"

"I knocked over my Mary statue in the middle of the night. I thought about what that girl said. I couldn't sleep, so I focused, and I made my leg move. I told it to move, and it did! I kicked it all night! I haven't slept. Somehow, my Mary statue on the windowsill fell over."

Mom's courageous heart moved her mountain that night with Mother Mary as a miraculous witness. For my mother, her darkest hours in fear ignited a surge of concentrated energy. Her determination, focus, faith, and courage, moved her leg and a wooden statue. Mom wasn't willing to believe in a limitation opined by a tech or a textbook.

Some say fear is the opposite of love. I disagree. Fear can be the motivator for self-love, preservation, and perseverance. Fear can activate the passion needed to push past the place of terror into triumph. Fear, when embraced with consciousness, can be harnessed as a tool for transformation.

Today, Mom is still mostly confined to her wheelchair, learning to live using the right side of her body. She still knows everyone she meets by name. We call her the mayor of her facility. She still has suitors who enjoy her company like catnip. Mom still sings her heart out…and sometimes even kicks her leg with the strength of a Radio City Rockette. She is still my greatest dance teacher.

Chapter *Fourteen*

Straight from the Snout: The Real Dish on Who Rescued Whom
By Lovey

Lovey

I write this under a pen name for my protection. You can call me "Lovey." I am a holistic chef with a BS in Holistic Nutrition, including natural pet care and holistic nutrition for companion animals. A certified IIN Health Coach, I am living the dream in the southwest. Friend to all dogs.

Straight from the Snout: The Real Dish on Who Rescued Whom
By Lovey

It is with three courageous hearts, honesty, integrity, and truth that I share with you this story of the divine love I still have for my two soul dogs, Monkey and Boo. It is written using my voice in the spirit of love and pure innocence that one can only guarantee from a dog, with forgiveness for myself, and with immense gratitude to North and Blue for rescuing me during our darkest hours.

Channeled and scribed with tears through the energetic spirit of my soul dogs' voices and a ministry of angels, we wish to deliver a message that resonates with you on a soul level. Maybe you too have had or are having this profound relationship, if not a telepathic form of communication, with your dogs that is so surreal, words can't describe it. An undying love, admiration, and affection that is so sacred you would have done anything for them—even sacrifice your soul. A spiritual connection they call divine love. It never gets old or dies.

There is no greater agony than bearing
an untold story inside you.

~ Maya Angelou

This is not a tell-all, and it's not to assassinate the character of anyone or to play the victim martyr. I am simply dying to use my voice and speak my truth. Perhaps this will touch your heartstrings and empower you not to make the same mistakes I did. I was originally going to write this story using a pen name for my protection. Then I realized, I want my power back. I am Joanie Veage. And I am using my voice to heal my heart and my soul.

Do not dim your light and stay too long.

Some people aren't going to like or accept this story. And that's okay. I'm telling it anyway. It's my story and my truth. I lived it. I own it. I forgive my past and continue to heal my grieving heart. I take full responsibility for my life—the good, the bad, and the ugly stuff. I know I am the co-creator of everything that has happened to and for me. What doesn't kill you makes you stronger. I would know.

You have to love yourself if you can ever *be* loved.

I married a man I barely knew. I was madly, deeply in love with him and I think he loved me too, in a weird kind of way. We were more like roommates, drinking buddies, then sparring partners for 25 years. We never met in the middle. I was never his number one. He wasn't emotionally available; he couldn't even look me in the eye. A master manipulator, psychologically abusive, and ever-humiliating when I opened my mouth or even dared to use my voice. A great escape artist who knew how to disappear a lot. I was starving for his love and affection. I was living a lie and putting on a good show for everyone. And the award goes to—

Less than three years into this marriage, I made a shocking discovery that altered my sanity for the next 22 years. I couldn't let it go; I wouldn't accept it. I thought there was something wrong with me. I hated myself and wanted to die. I became extremely angry and took it out on everyone. I especially took my pain, agony, and suffering out on the one person I truly admired and loved more than life itself—my sister. Today I call her Baby B. I bore that shame and agony for decades. Today, it is her forgiveness that most feeds my soul and heals my heart.

Upon this discovery, I began to heavily abuse my body, mind, and soul with a lot of cocaine and alcohol—a lot. This would cause a nervous breakdown, forcing me to leave the best job I ever had, and, believing something was wrong with me, a world concert tour seeking medical help and a psychiatrist. My strong survival instinct kicked in, and I recovered quickly. Or so I thought.

This was not a marriage. It was a karmic contract.

I returned to work and was partly shunned. I didn't know how to ask for help or use my voice then. It cost me the best friends I ever had. I felt alone. And from that episode, moving forward, my life would be forever changed. I went through many years of evolving, both personally and professionally, in an effort to fix my marriage and reinvent myself. Hello, therapy!

When someone is acting crazy or believes that they're crazy, it can be a telltale sign they're in an abusive relationship.

Moving forward a decade, I continued touring on and off. I graduated from culinary school and opened a successful catering company. Then, in 2001, due to irreconcilable differences, I filed for a divorce for the first time, but didn't see it through. I still loved my husband and continued to think there was something wrong with me. He bought me a big house. I stayed in therapy and kept living a lie that continued to rob my soul and my sanity. The defining moments and beginning of the end of this karmic contract and the hell that was to come started, coupled with the greatest love affair I've ever had. The love and life I shared with my soul dogs for those 13-plus years were simply divine.

And so it was that Monkey and Boo came into my life in early 2000 and rescued me. Soon after, I semi-retired from the music biz, and finally felt I had real love and joy in my life. FYI—I picked Monkey, but Boo picked me. I was Boo's human. We were a pack of three, practically joined at the hip our entire lives together and separated only a few times.

Soon after, I had an opportunity to buy a restaurant that I frequented and absolutely loved. I thought this would be a good fit for my family and lifestyle and would be a huge success. My husband and I bought that restaurant. However, he was diametrically opposed to this business, and his unforgiven resentment and utter hatred for me catapulted. I was soon cut off from any affection, constantly humiliated, threatened that my dogs and I would be put on the street, and almost tricked into selling my house for one dollar so he could run away and flee the country. Which he eventually did.

Like those who have children, I was now instilled with an immense fear of abandonment that tortured me for the next ten years. I had no more self-esteem or confidence. I was mentally exhausted and operating on fear, which got me more of the same. How would I survive and take care of my dogs? It made me flipping crazy. I could not function. I was a total bitch to everyone—especially my employees. I lost total control of myself and lost my restaurant.

I now ask for forgiveness for being such a kitchen bitch—I mean, Hell's Kitchen style. I am not that person today, by the way.

Moving forward, my dogs were my only real comfort. We had an extraordinary, deep, and meaningful form of telepathic communication that not everyone has or would understand. We had our own language. I felt their love. We had a lot of friends and people we trail-walked and hiked with, neighbors we came to love, and a new group of friends in the local animal rescue community. I was mostly working from home, as well as studying for my master's in Holistic Nutrition, and taking a few tours here and there. The dogs were my life and joy.

Monkey and Boo, being inner-breed Labs, came with a lot of health problems that no conventional vet could ever help me with. By three years of age, these health problems created exhausting challenges for me—Monkey's poor bone health and cancer, immunity issues and allergies that catapulted Boo's hair loss, 24/7 itching, vomiting, grand mal seizures, complete airway constriction, and asthma. One day, thank *Dog*, a friend of mine stopped by the house to pick up some soup. She was a first-responder in the medical profession, and from the corner of her eye, she recognized that Boo was having a silent asthma attack. She saved his life with pet CPR. Not kidding—had she not been there, he would have crossed that rainbow bridge that night. Days later, I became certified in pet CPR and found a holistic vet who would change our lives forever.

While my dogs had many hiccups after that, they survived and thrived using natural pet care and holistic nutrition. I went on to finish my BS in Holistic Nutrition, including holistic nutrition and certification in natural pet care for companion animals. I was a contributing writer to a local-regional pet-friendly magazine and many other local public-ations. I fostered special needs dogs, started a personal chef service and a home-cooked pet food business, volunteered at my local Humane Society, shelters, and pet charities, ran shelter dogs on the weekends, and made blankets for shelter cats and dogs. North and Blue made me a better person and helped to change the trajectory of my life and perception.

I also caused more hatred and alienation of affection towards me from my husband. I tried to get the courage to leave again in late 2008 by filing for a divorce a second time, but changed my mind. In the years that followed, I discovered my entire investment account was withdrawn behind my back. Then my entire savings. And it's a devastating betrayal to find out your husband has built himself a beautiful home in his name only. He was getting his ducks in a row to abandon my dogs and me. Now cash-poor, I felt even more helpless and hopeless, isolated, and still living in fear of the abandonment I knew was coming. So, I stayed put until that pending day of departure. The years that followed were inconceivably demoralizing and getting physically abusive.

You can steal my money, but not my joy.

By 2014, my partner's resentment for me catapulted to absolutely crazy, terrifying, and disgusting. My mother suddenly became ill and soon after passed away. Ninety minutes before my flight to New York for her wake and funeral, he threatened to leave home and desert my dogs—abandon them. I didn't make that flight. Thank *Dog* I had Monkey's and Boo's love. I wanted to die that day. Ten years of threats of abandonment had sucked the life out of me. I never got to say goodbye to my beautiful, angelic mother, and I also made another shocking discovery and was warned not to talk.

You know what happens to whistleblowers, Joan. I'll take you down.

Again, I wanted to die. Days later, my husband left home and never came back to us. Months later, my father passed away. Boo was diagnosed with cancer, but survived his surgery and recovered. I was hit with divorce papers and ordered to sell and leave my home. I was terrorized and threatened that if I did not sell to the first buyer, I would be institutionalized for a mental evaluation and my dogs taken from me.

I sold out and gave almost everything I owned away. The dogs and I moved into the only house with a yard that would have us, where I would be stalked by a crazy neighbor. Five months later, I walked away from that house with the clothes on my back and two extremely sick dogs. That house and the toxic mold could have killed us. We had to live in hotels for a few months because we had nowhere else to go. Most people repelled us once we became needy and helpless. That, too, sucked.

While I was working 14 hours a day, those courageous dogs had to be quarantined for 12 hours a day at a vet's office. They would cry all day and knowing that almost killed me. I started losing 40% of my hair, my teeth were breaking, I had brain fog, memory loss, and a lot of accidents. A hair analysis report showed that I also had heavy metal poisoning, which I already knew.

If not for the courageous hearts of those dogs, I may not be sitting here writing this story. The dogs gave me the will to survive attempts at suicide. They left for the rainbow bridge in early 2016. Monkey suddenly crossed, and Boo lost his will to live. It was tragic. While I was secretly suicidal, I took a leap of faith and attended my first spiritual conference in Phoenix. The serendipities and synergistic events that occurred during those few days in Phoenix will forever be the defining moment that literally changed my mind and my life. I surrendered to my higher power and that of the universal energy field. I started taking a spiritual path with regular meditation, daily affirmations, and mantras. I found out that there's nothing wrong with me—it's a human condition. Oh, and I'm an empath.

I found my soul tribe and a ministry of angels. I am no longer walking alone. Thank you, Cookie Fudge. Today, I am the happiest I've ever been. I think about Monkey and Boo every day of my life. Today, I have finally experienced divine love for another human being—you know who you are. Wow! It feels good. I'm living with an attitude of gratitude. Living the dream, as I say every day of my life. I have peace of mind. I am healthy. I am abundant in every way. I am a career success thanks to three bitches—dogs, that is. I have a beautiful home, and I even share some time with a miniature horse on occasion.

Divine love—it's all you need.

Chapter

Fifteen

Courageous Hearts, Acts of Resistance

By Anne Mackie Morelli

Anne Mackie Morelli

Anne Mackie Morelli, BPE, MA, RCC, is a former Canadian national track and field champion, Olympian, educator, clinical counselor, and pastor, who is now spending her time writing and speaking. She is a woman of faith who has been profoundly impacted by God's radical love and grace. Anne is currently enrolled in the seminary at Trinity Western University, in Langley, British Columbia, Canada, where she is completing a Master's Degree in Christian Studies and Leadership. Her first solo book, When Grief Descends: Suffering, Consolation, and The Book of Job, became an international bestseller when it was first published in June 2020 by As You Wish Publishing.

Anne and her husband have been married for 43 years. They have three grown sons, now all married, and four grandsons. Anne is passionate about empowering others to use their talents, strengths, and leadership abilities for the greater good and to effect positive change in their families, communities, and the world around them. She believes that with encouragement and support, every individual has the capacity to contribute and to lead wherever God has placed them. Follow or contact Anne through her website, https://www.annemackiemorelli.com,
Twitter @EAnneMorelli,
Facebook @AnneMackieMorelliwriter.

Courageous Hearts, Acts of Resistance
By Anne Mackie Morelli

Corruption and immorality had insidiously woven themselves into the culture. Tensions were high as people were becoming polarized. Most were holding tight to one viewpoint or another. Disrespect, discord, and conflicts had escalated. People were becoming increasingly afraid to speak up or protest against corruption because of how it stirred up threats and persecution in response. The way through the tensions seemed obscured and shrouded with obstacles. Trust had evaporated. Peaceful resolutions seemed increasingly elusive. "There is no win-win scenario in this chapter: the stakes—political, personal, and theological—[were] simply too high."[1]

The leadership and its supporting cast were characterized by a despotic, immoral use of power. While many did not support the regime, there seemed no clear way to break the chokehold they had on power. In contrast, a significant portion of the population revered and defended the leadership. As a result, enough of the population was willing to ignore or overlook the tyrannical leadership and embrace their falsehoods and biases. It was this base of supporters who enabled the leadership to execute their devious schemes.

While these circumstances sound familiar to what we are currently observing in many countries around the world, this is actually recounting a specific narrative and a dark period in ancient Judah. And though this ancient biblical chronicle does not reveal immediate, specific, step-by-step directions that might help us to navigate our way through such current world circumstances, it does illuminate certain cross-cultural and timeless truths that can encourage and provide hope. This specific tale affirms that even small acts of courageous resistance have the potential to subvert dark circumstances and exert influence on how events evolve.

This ancient biblical account focuses on the corrupt authority of the royal leadership and the heroic actions of two women who bravely made a decision to rise up against it. Their swift thinking and daring actions not only subverted the Queen's formidable and immoral leadership, but their actions ultimately influenced the destiny of their nation and the future of the following generations.

The narrative includes three extremely different women—Queen Athaliah, Princess Jehosheba, and an unnamed wet-nurse. While this episode is set within the arc of God's grand, eternal narrative, its immediate backdrop was one of ancient political turmoil, the contrasts of good and evil, justice and injustice, and "the political and theological vacillation of the people" [2] (2 Kings 11 and 2 Chronicles 22-23). These three women were embroiled in this struggle between good and evil, and each had to make a decision about how they were going to respond to the events going on around them.

Athaliah was the daughter of King Ahab and Queen Jezebel, and the granddaughter of Omri (one of the most idolatrous and wicked kings of that era). Athaliah was born into a period where the majority of people worshipped idols and denied God. She had married Jehoram, the firstborn of

Judah's godly king Jehosophat for political purposes and to cement an alliance between the northern and southern kingdoms. [3] "When Jehoram assumed the throne in 849 B.C.E., he put all his brothers and some princes of Israel to the sword; significantly, they were all [followers of God]." [4] As Athaliah became the "power behind the throne," her worship of idols influenced her husband and their people away from following God, towards worshipping idols.[5] After eight years, her husband Jehoram died, and her son Ahaziah became king. But within a little over a year, he was slain by Jehu, the king of the Northern Kingdom of Israel. Upon hearing about her son's death, Athaliah immediately seized the throne and ordered the slaughter of all the remaining male heirs in the royal family (2 Kings 11:1; 2 Chronicles 22:10-11).

Once Athaliah became the "power on the throne," the length of her six-year reign testified to her determination, heartlessness, and intelligence.[6] A despotic ruler, she ensured that her every command was obeyed. The fact she was the only woman to have ever ruled in ancient Judah is a statement about her ruthlessness and her "control of the religious establishment."[7]

While scripture itself does not reveal her specific motives for the murder of the royal heirs, scholars have proposed differing explanations for why she sought to execute all the male descendants. The interpretations have suggested that she coveted power, had an opportunistic nature, was envious of the royal heirs, it was a political purge of her rivals, she feared for her life, and she sought to eradicate the Davidic line from which Jesus would eventually come.[8]

Regardless, the slaughter of her grandchildren, all royal heirs, does highlight how "she put the whole nation under the shadow of a great horror. She trampled on all faith. She lived outside the law. She violated all obligation. She lived with the shrieks of those she butchered in her ears. She lived with her hands red with the blood of princes and princesses."[9] The murders of her family members and her subsequent rule further contributed to the country's political and theological deterioration.[10]

In the narrative, the two other women are introduced as minor or secondary characters, but because of their daring, they ended up influencing how this story concluded. The first woman was Jehosheba, a king's daughter and the sister of King Ahaziah, who was married to the high priest, Jehoiada. The second woman, who remained unnamed, was a wet-nurse who had been hired to breastfeed and care for the youngest royal heir, Joash. While these two women wielded no official or sanctioned authority, they opted to use the little influence they did have. They chose to remain faithful to the Lord and to the moral standard he expected. As a result, they refused to engage with the rampant corruption or bow to the immoral authority of the Queen and those who supported her, even when their choice placed them in mortal danger.

As all the king's male descendants were being slaughtered, Jehosheba made a choice to subvert this reign of terror. Acting decisively, she scooped up Joash, the youngest son of Ahaziah, to save him from the "orgy of destruction" (2 Kings 11:2-3).[11] Once she spirited the one-year-old royal baby away, she concealed him and his wet nurse in one of the temple rooms, and then for the next six years, she kept him hidden in the temple (2 Kings 11:3; 2 Chronicles 22:11-12). [12] The temple was an ideal hiding spot, because Queen Athaliah, an idol worshipper, was unlikely to stumble upon the heir's presence in this holy place. Hiding Joash in the temple also ensured that the young heir could be tutored in the ways of the Lord. After seven tense years, the high priest, Jehoiada, and the captains of the guard brought the boy out of hiding and anointed the young heir as king. Queen Athaliah was finally overthrown and put to death (2 Kings 11:4-12).

Jehosheba's subversive act of rescuing the youngest heir and protecting him for six years ultimately led to the end of Athaliah's rule and her attempts to eradicate the royal lineage. Her quick thinking and courageous heart had preserved the line from which the Messiah would eventually come.[13] Unfortunately, while the young King Joash began his reign with worthy intentions and was initially obedient to God's will, he quickly succumbed to temptations and to wickedness.

This pattern of power and leadership, shifting back and forth between faithfulness and disobedience, highlights how humans continue to wrestle with good and evil. In hindsight, we can easily discern how this struggle has been woven throughout theological, economic, political, and human narratives over the centuries. Even today, we continue to be faced with daily decisions that require us to decide between what is right and wrong, and which path we are ultimately going take. And each decision that we make will propel us down one of two primary paths, with each choice and its outcomes, becoming knitted into our personal stories.

Whenever a decision must be made, everything essentially boils down to two primary themes. It is like we are standing at a crossroads and facing the prospect of having to take one of two paths. One path will lead us towards God and what is true and fair. The other path will lead us away from God and towards what is immoral and false and unholy. When we truly think about it, almost every decision boils down to these distinctive core themes—the choices between moral and immoral, light and darkness, justice and injustice, love and hate.

It is tempting to think that if we delay and do not affirm a choice, we will be saved from having to take a stand and declare what we believe is right or wrong. But in reality, remaining quiet, standing by, and simply watching are all momentous choices. For what we can often overlook, is that when we refuse to make a decision or speak out, we are actually choosing. We are casting our voting for the status quo to continue. We are endorsing whatever is transpiring. And as we sit on the sidelines, we are complicit in allowing others to move their agendas forward and write the storyline.

Oftentimes we are tempted to complain about what is going on and are quick to criticize others. And while we grumble, the leaders and their followers continue to hold power and determine outcomes. Other times, as we argue and debate about which is the best route, we can get stuck at the crossroads. But as we stand and complain and quarrel, we end up missing the opportunities to initiate change.

We can also be lulled into thinking that only highly conspicuous and impressive acts of resistance have the power to defeat or overcome corrupt authority. Believing there is no way that we could make a difference, we give up.

But whenever we linger too long at the crossroads, we will end up becoming the supporting cast.

Yet, a cross-cultural and timeless truth conveyed through this ancient biblical chronicle is that, even those of us who do not have official status or authority, do have the power to activate positive change and subvert a storyline. Whenever anyone of us chooses to inject God's love and truth into dark spaces, there is the potential to overcome it. When we are willing to partner with God, either as an individual or as a collective body, we unleash his love into the world so that the trajectory of these types of events can be transformed into what is good and decent and right. Whenever we are like Jehosheba and the nurse, and courageously accept the invitation to rise, it becomes possible to snap the inertia and initiate positive momentum.

As Jehosheba scooped up her nephew Joash, I don't imagine she had much time to consider what her actions might cost her or what might happen next. She did not have the time to stand at the crossroads and debate what might be the best route for her to take. She merely took the first step. Likewise, in difficult circumstances, we too are called to move, take the initial step, and move towards what is worthy—not trying to play it too safe, or taking the time to overthink, or being overly worried about the subsequent steps or where the path might end up leading. In faith, we are invited to start by making a decision that takes us and others towards what is right. Doing the honorable things that allow us to participate in God's kingdom work and help to move his eternal narrative forward.

But we can be assured that whenever we are faced with making a decision that may have us stepping into the unknown or the scary or the unimaginable, we are never alone. God promises to be with us when we walk along the narrow path. He will equip, sustain, provide for, and protect his people.

We can also be assured that when leaders, like Queen Athaliah, choose to misuse their power and attempt to eradicate what is noble and true, God will triumph in the end. We know this to be true because, in Scripture, we see God's faithfulness to his people over and over and over again.

I imagine that these two women never dreamed of how their actions would end up changing the course of history, or how they would be featured in the Bible and read about for thousands of years afterward. Yet, their courage is still being acknowledged thousands of years later.

Each of us is called to be decisive in such critical moments of time—to be like Jehosheba and Joash's unnamed caregiver. To be willing to make decisions that reflect what is beneficial and fair and good. To bravely take that first step, shining light into the dark spaces, so that the hard and the harmful can be shifted and transformed, becoming people whose courageous hearts and bold initiatives map nobler directions, and charting pathways that become illuminated by love, justice, and decency.

Endnotes:

[1] Robin Gallaher Branch. Jeroboam's Wife: The Enduring Contributions of the Old Testament's Least-known Women. (Grand Rapids, Michigan: Baker Academic, 2009), 156-157.

[2] Ibid, 151.

[3] Dorothy Patterson and Rhonda Harrington Kelley, eds. The Woman's Study Bible. (Nashville, TE: Thomas Nelson, 2006) 488.

[4] Branch, 152.

[5] Herbert Lockyer. All the Women of the Bible, (Grand Rapids, Michigan: Zondervan,1967), 33.

[6] Ibid, 33.

[7] Williams E. Phipps. Assertive Biblical Women, (Westport, Connecticut: Greenwood Press, 1992), 78.

[8] Branch, 159. Ann Spangler and Jean E. Syswerda. Women of the Bible: A One-Year Devotional Study of Women in Scripture, (Grand Rapids, Michigan: Zondervan, 2007), 235; Edith Dean. All the Women of the Bible (New York: Castle Books, 1995), 141. Tikva Frymer-Kensky. Reading the Women of the Bible (New York: Schocken Books, 2002), 86.

[9] Lockyer, 33.

[10] Branch, 159.

[11] Lockyer, 33.

[12] Carol L. Meyers, Toni Craven, and Ross S. Kraemer. Women in Scripture: a Dictionary of Named and Unnamed Women in the Hebrew Bible, the Apocryphal / Deuterocanonical Books, and the New Testament. (Grand Rapid, Michigan: Williams B. Eerdmans Publishing, 2000) 277.

Chapter

Sixteen

The Power of Being
By James Masters

James Masters

James attended seminary to become a full-time minister-pastor, but eventually, the God of his understanding became more expansive and inclusive than the God of his religion. This led him on a journey of spiritual self-discovery.

As his insights and spiritual path progressed, he became a full-time intuitive coach in 2012. That has been his primary focus for several years. He currently has four primary services in his spiritual and metaphysical practice:

Emotional Freedom Technique (EFT) and Thought Field Therapy (TFT) coaching, intuitive art, intuitive readings, and Spirit Guidance Coaching.

His four-week EFT/TFT program called "Tapping into Joy" is focused on freeing up stuck energy that can stop individuals from living their full and joyous potential.

The intuitive art service is a creative practice that provides clients with a deeper understanding of metaphysics and their spiritual connection through visual imagery and interpretation. Intuitive readings are one-time sessions that are meant to encourage, guide, and provide answers to questions clients have about their lives.

Finally, Spirit Guidance Coaching is a program designed to help others tap into their individual intuitive center. This is a six-week program that covers a variety of topics such as symbolic spiritual language, archetypes, synchronicity, angels, guides, and much more.

Some of his artwork is available on his website as prints, there may even be an original thrown in here and there. If you click on the "musing" section of the website, you can learn the meaning and messages behind these pictures.

You can find out more by visiting www.jamesmasters.net, or on Facebook at www.facebook.com/jamesdmastersjr.

The Power of Being
by James Masters

I was recently asked by a teacher to consider the difference between *being* and *becoming*. I appreciated this inquiry because the same day it was presented to me, I had written a poem entitled, "Behold, All Things Become New," which you will find at the end of this chapter. The poem was all about *being*.

I had developed a habit of *becoming*, which in retrospect, caused me to leave out some deeply meaningful experiences of life. By the time my teacher's question came up, I had already realized that my *becoming* was becoming an exhausting experience. The need to *become* can take away from the present moment of *being*.

As an intuitive coach, I have worked from a home office for years. I still participated in events and classes outside of the house, but my main "work" hub was in a home office. In my office, I have always used a whiteboard to identify and work through goals. For years it has been filled with all kinds of things. Writing, art, social media presence, marketing, events, meetings, and other *to do's* that would help me in my *becoming*.

Several global and personal events caused me to evaluate how I was investing my time and energy. My goals were never-ending. I would finish one project, only to see another emerge. I would accomplish one goal, only to see two more replace it.

Even before this question about *becoming* and *being* came to me, I had already cleared out the whiteboard. I reached a point where I needed to settle down and allow myself to be. So, I erased the whiteboard, wrote a poem, and the question from my teacher emerged. I took my whiteboard and wrote in big letters: "Goals: Be."

I posted it on my social media page and then decided to sit for a while. I was not sure for how long I was going to sit with it, but I figured that I would sit for as long as it took for the exhaustion and stress to dissipate.

After posting this to my social media account, I noticed that I received mixed responses. Some people said, "It's about time." Those were people that knew me extremely well. Others could not conceptualize what it meant. I had one friend say, "I had to think about this for a while. I kept seeing '*Goals: Beryllium.*'" As I engaged with the comments and then released them, the thought of making my goal in life to simply *be* ended up feeling like a revolutionary act.

I have done centering practices for years. However, those practices were always associated with my goals and one of the "to do" elements of my day. Yoga, check. Meditate, check. EFT, check. Journaling, check. Pray, check. This worked well for quite some time. I studied centering practices, and my list of practices kept growing. When I erased the whole list and allowed myself to *be,* I recognized that this was a different type of experience altogether.

My lists and my desire to *become* never allowed me to just *be.* I do not believe this was bad or wrong. I was a product of my society and culture. I remember being asked as a child, "What do you want to *be* when you grow up?" I could never develop a clear answer to this question. I do not think I ever wanted to grow up. Eventually, I did buy into the practice of *becoming,* and it served me for many years. However, when I chose to let myself *be* for a while, without something to achieve, I felt vulnerable.

This entire book is about courage, and I want to point out that in my experience, just being takes tremendous courage. As I focused on this new goal of *being,* I realized how tyrannous my desire to *become* had *become.*

The first things that came to mind were all the deadlines. Who will pay the bills? Who will water the plants? Who will write the manuscript? Who will attend the meetings? Who will paint the pictures? Who will run the meetings? *Becoming* carried with it a lot of anxiety and stress and *being* brought all those things to the surface.

Question after question emerged in my mind, and each time, I had to give those questions over to Love and allow God to sustain me in them. More than questions came up as I allowed myself to *be.* I was faced with insecurities and emotions that I had not recognized on the journey of *becoming.*

With each question that came up, I allowed myself to simply *be* with the questions. I listened to the messages I had been putting out in the world for the past decade. I have been encouraging people to trust, breathe, and know that there is a Loving Intelligence that supports us. My messages were deeply authentic, but when I stopped and allowed myself to be present, I realized that I had not always been faithful to my words. Sure, I trusted that the Divine Source would provide, but I also believed that I had to work at it.

Someone recently reminded me that there is a lie in the middle of everything we beLIEve. Yes, this is true. As the metaphysical text known as the Kybalion says, "All truths are half-truths." We can only see life through the lens of our experiences. So now it's time to practice.

Who will pay the bills? The angels are paying the bills. Who will water the plants? God will water the plants. Who will write the manuscript? Love will write the manuscript. Who will attend the meetings? God will need to figure that part out. For right now, I need to let myself *be.*

This choice to allow myself to *be* was an opportunity for me to give all these questions to this Divine Loving Intelligence and practice trusting and knowing.

A second component came up as well. Prior to setting this goal, I had someone say to me, "You need to ask for help." Then, after a few days of allowing myself *to be*, my teacher made the same suggestion. The idea to ask for help caused me to feel vulnerable, but finally reached a point where I decided to ask for help. That day I said to my husband, "I think I am going to ask for help."

He said, "Good. I've never heard you ask for help." When I realized the truth of his words, a wave of emotion washed over me, and I cried. I have always focused on holding it all together and doing things by myself. Clearly, that strategy was not helping my ability to *be*, so there must *be* another way.

I did not know where to ask for help, so at first, I asked everyone I could think of that might be able to help. I did not get many answers, but that was okay. I viewed the process as putting out seeds everywhere. As a gardener, I realize that

I cannot grow flowers. I can only plant seeds, water them, and then some other Force grows them.

Each time I put out a request for help, I simply went back to allowing Divine Intelligence to sustain me. I would sit and be. I came across a line from *A Course in Miracles* in Dr. Robert Holden's book *Lovability* that says it all, "Love always answers, being unable to deny a call for help." I spent a whole day contemplating these words.

The questions continued to rise and fall along with my emotions. With each one, I moved my attention to trusting that there is a Divine Intelligence working everything out. I focused on breathing and trusting. Eventually, I felt wonderfully comfortable with the smaller questions, things like, "who will feed the cat." When this question came up, I would look at the cat dish, noticed if it needed to be filled, and if it did, I would fill it. If it did not, I would let it go.

Questions of the world eventually emerged. For many years I have dedicated my energy to creating a more equitable and loving society. I have volunteered at homeless shelters. I have protested injustice. I have held up signs. I have worked with people one on one and in groups. I handed out *positive affirmation* cards to nearly everyone I met. I know some of you reading this have received one of these cards, and I want to say thank you for your loving support in purchasing this book.

When this new question about *being and becoming* came to me, it was during the time of Covid19. It was during the time of social distancing. It was during the time of mass protests in the streets for racial and economic justice. Each time I checked in with this new goal of *being*, I realized that it was not time for me to go protest, hold up signs, lie down in the streets, or even hand out cards. It was time to let myself *be* and observe what was unfolding.

I started handing that over as well. Who will feed the homeless? The other angels on our planet will feed the homeless. Who will march in the streets? God will fill the streets. Who will run the campaign? God will care for the systems.

I chose to have confidence that when it was time for me to move, I would move out of my *being* rather than out of a need to *become*. I did not need to save the world. The more I allowed myself to be, the more I realized that the world was holding together quite nicely without my assistance.

The final questions that came up were probably the most difficult. As I realized that there was nothing that needed me to do anything, a sense of dread came over me. The thought, "The world doesn't need you," started coming to mind.

This brought up several of my existential concerns. Whether or not my life had value or meaning. Whether or not I had been doing the *right* thing with my life. Other concerns started emerging, but I can sum these up simply, they were the voice of my ego, saying, "You're not good enough."

At first, I attempted to think my way out of these concerns. I have been doing spiritual practices long enough to know that I do not have to believe everything I think, and I do not have to make myself or others wrong or bad. One thing I am certain of is that it is Love that holds all of this together. Love is the path that we are on, and it is the destination. It was clear that these were all old messages that were stuck in my psyche. Many of them were childhood traumas that I had never fully resolved.

Thankfully, I had the resources and understanding to know what to do. I got out my hand-held mirror, and I started saying, "James, I love you just the way you are." If you have never done this before, I would highly recommend it. In her book, "Mirror Work," Louise Hay discusses how the mirror does not judge us. If we see something in the mirror that we do not like, it is something that we are doing to ourselves.

I had done mirror work for years, but this time it felt different. I had done a great job in dealing with patterns regarding physical features, but doing mirror work as a process of allowing myself to *be* rather than as something to help me become opened up an entirely new avenue of self-discovery.

If you ever decide to do this practice, I highly recommend bringing some tissues along with you. There I was, sitting in front of the mirror and allowing myself to *be*. A resentment would come up, I would do some forgiveness. A particular fear would come up, I would do some forgiveness. Blame toward myself or others would come up, I would do some forgiveness. Feelings of guilt would come up; I would do some forgiveness. Criticisms and judgments would come up, I would do some forgiveness.

Eventually, nothing came up. I could only see myself in the mirror. I had been saying the affirmation, "I do not need to earn love, I am lovable because I exist," for years! Now, in this state of allowing myself to be, it was not only a thought floating around in my mind. It became my reality.

I sat there for a good long while. Purely appreciating and being. Then, I stood up and went to my yoga mat and did some yoga. No music, no timers, nothing. Only the mat, myself, and yoga. Then I picked up a book and read a bit of it. Then I watered the flowers. I went for a walk and sat under a tree for a long time. I looked up at the sky, I appreciated the earth under me, supporting me and sustaining me. Then I sat down at my computer to write, and here we are together. Not needing to *become* anything, but just being and moving from the heart.

One time I heard Dr. Wayne Dyer say, "God writes all the books. God builds all the bridges. God produces all the plays and stars in them. God paints all the pictures." There is a place within each of us that many traditions call *spirit.* I believe that it is a place within our hearts that is connected to Divine Creative Intelligence. Within this space, everything is already accomplished. We do not need to become something, because in this place we already are something.

It is the place where we can let ourselves breathe, trust, know, and *be*. In this place, all is well.

Behold, All Things Become New

Be.

It is true

Be is the beginning of bewilderment.

It is true

That be is the beginning of behaviors.

The beginning of becoming.

True still be is the beginning of beginnings.

The beginning of beholding.

The beginning of benevolence.

Of belonging.

Be is the beginning of believing.

I've even found That be can be the beginning of inquiry.

"To be or not to be?" As they say.

But most importantly Be is the beginning of BECAUSE

And because

Be the beginning of beauty.

It must be alright

To simply

Be.

Chapter *Seventeen*

Dancing To My Own Rhythm

By Sarah E. McArthur

Sarah E. McArthur

Sarah E. McArthur is a certified aroma freedom practitioner, an intuitive life coach, an author, a speaker, and a former Executive Director of Impact Personal Safety of Colorado. Her passion for empowering others to live their most authentic and free lives was birthed out of the wisdom she learned on her healing journey. Her life was transformed by Impact Personal Safety of Colorado almost ten years ago, and she has dedicated herself to helping others experience empowerment, personal safety, and healing. Within the last few years, Sarah has become a certified aroma freedom practitioner, using aromatherapy to help herself and others experience emotional release from past experiences and pain so that they can find their life's natural flow.

Sarah E. McArthur can be reached through her website: www.sarahemcarthur.com.

I would like to thank everyone in my life who loves me for who I truly am!

Dancing To My Own Rhythm
By Sarah E. McArthur

If you asked me what living with a courageous heart meant a few months ago, my answer would have been different than it is now. I often think of concepts like courage as a big gesture or the ultimate action. If the stakes are high enough, then it's quite noticeable and awesome when I "achieve" courage. "Look how courageous I was when I—," followed by whatever it was I did. When I decided to write this chapter, I was living in that big gesture space. I was "achieving" my courage and making big strides past my life-long struggle with fear paralysis. Fear paralysis is the term I use because I have let fear stop me from taking steps forward in my life many times; in fact, too many times.

Let me share with you some of the big gestures I made to face my fears in the last year. I participated in a collaborative book and became a published author for the first time. I was scared to write, and I did it anyway. I pursued a life dream and participated in a book signing at Barnes and Noble. I was scared, and I did it anyway. I spoke at a conference in Nashville, Tennessee, for International Women's Day. My fear had me so nervous that I don't remember everything I said. I was scared, and I did it anyway. I am an entrepreneur, and through a series of opportunities, I became an events manager. I was asked to manage an event in Las Vegas. Previously, my other events were local in Colorado, so this was next-level for me. I was scared, and I did it anyway. I signed up to attend level-one self-defense training in Israel with ESD Global. It had been a long time since I traveled overseas, I am afraid of flying, and I was taking my nine-year-old son with me. I was scared, and I did it anyway.

I was making all the big gestures to achieve my courage. I am not discounting the fact that it took a lot of courage to step into these experiences, it truly did. It's just not the full story of my life. It's a version of the story that shows my best foot forward. The story I want to tell is one where courage is not only in the big strides, but in smaller ones, including rest. My deeper courage comes from my willingness to face the truth—the whole truth. It's being willing to look at the stories I tell myself and the deeper truth behind them. It's my willingness to look at my strengths and my weaknesses. It's about my ability to shine bright and my ability to plunge into the darkness of my deep sorrow. Speaking about my truth so candidly makes me want to stop writing right now. It stirs my deepest insecurities. It awakens that inner voice that reminds me that I can be judged and deemed "not enough" or "broken."

I am not a therapist or doctor. I am definitely not an expert on any topic, but I know my life, my lessons, and the wisdom I have picked up along the way. My greatest intent in telling pieces of my story is to let you know you are not alone in your rise to success or in the shadows of your pain. I have been in both places, in the past and in the present. Life is complex. I think since I first realized this, I try to be kinder to myself and others. I try to judge less, love more, accept more, and hold more space for others. Do I always get it right? Not at all, but I try.

My life history is complex, confusing, and riddled with paralyzing fear, pain, and trauma. I have always struggled to find ways to succinctly talk about it. There are so many aspects, so many different stories that I never know where to start or where to end. I have found that frequently my whole story can be overwhelming and hard to process. I used to believe that I had to tell all of it for others to connect. I have found that to not be true. I can share as much or little as I feel comfortable with at the moment because I am sharing from my heart. I am giving the gift of vulnerability and courage.

Some days I feel like I have come so far in my healing, and other days I wonder if I have healed at all. The recent worldwide experience of Covid-19 is a good example of this. Prior to the spread of Covid-19 in the United States, I was achieving all the things mentioned above. I felt like I was taking big strides in overcoming the fear of putting myself out there to be seen and potentially judged by others, which is no easy feat for me. Finally, I was overcoming these feelings. When local governments began implanting restrict-ions, those courageous feelings went out the window quickly. An old, familiar, heavy cloud of anxiety and fear settled in.

Anxiety and fear tend to ebb and flow throughout my life. I used to want to heal so I can be "rid" of them, but repeatedly found myself feeling defeated. Then I would become angry with myself in the process for not being able to get "rid" of them. I am much gentler with myself now. I now realize courage isn't only about not experiencing or facing my anxiety and fear again. It's not about ignoring it either. It's about becoming aware of it, seeing it, acknowledging its presence, and becoming more aware that I need to be gentler with myself right now. This is not the time for me to make the big gestures of courage. It's the time for me to make all the little ones that add up to living in presence and truth.

I previously mentioned that I am an event planner, but like most things in my life, my work life is also complex. I am an adult with ADHD, so variety suits me well. It makes complete sense to me that I wouldn't have one career path. I have many. On top of event planning, I am also a healing practitioner and life coach. I also have ten years' experience in empowerment self-defense and still work in that field. When I think about these different paths, I am truly amazed that each one found me. I wasn't looking to become an event planner, a healer, or a self-defense instructor. All I did was take one step after the other in their direction. This, to me, is a key—one step at a time. Sometimes the step is forward, sometimes it is backward, sometimes it's to the side, and sometimes it's back to the center.

If you haven't noticed by now, I can be action-oriented. So, when I say one step, my mind shouts, "Take a huge productive step," while my heart whispers, "Do what you need to be okay in this moment." I have powered through numerous, "I am not okay," moments that ended in big crashes, the soul-exhausted kind of crash. I use the term soul-exhausted because it describes how I feel when I have been going against my flow for so long that even my soul is exhausted and it feels like I can't take another step. It's like walking in a river against the current—at some point I will become so exhausted that I can't keep going. I have begun to learn that a tiny step is still a step, and it still takes courage. Sometimes that step is acknowledging that I am not okay today, and telling someone so I am not isolating. Sometimes that tiny step is giving myself permission to stay in bed and binge-watch TV. Sometimes it's sitting in the shower and crying because I feel too much, too often. Facing my truths, that is the deeper courage.

I'd like to say that I no longer tell myself that I am broken, but in my hard moments, I still do. I still struggle with insecurity. I struggle with self-doubt. Impostor syndrome is alive and well in my life. No matter how many times I have successfully done something, I will still convince myself I can't do it again. It might seem paradoxical when you read some of my accomplishments in the last year. I can assure you that it is always a process for me to get where I am going. On the path to accomplishment, my journey can be filled with self-doubt and reminders of how "not enough," I think I am. I am learning to take one step at a time and be okay. Frequently when I speak with clients, in my healing practice, we examine the word okay. "Okay" feels so bland, like a saltine cracker with no salt. Have you ever had one? No, thank you, yuck. Okay, feels too grey, too neutral, and not good enough. We want all or nothing, and I have found that few are okay with being just okay.

Being okay helps me to find my footing. It gives me a starting place. What do I need to be okay right now? Do I need help? Do I need sleep? Do I need rest? Do I need a friend? Do I need a hug? Do I need to focus on a project? If I want to know where I am going, I have to know where I am starting. Okay helps me determine my starting point. I am learning to be okay with my capacities. I have the capacity to achieve great things, and I have the capacity to achieve nothing because I need to focus on just being okay. Both are part of me, and I am learning to be okay with both.

As I learn to accept these truths about myself, I can give myself more kindness when the struggle is deeper. Self-compassion is truly powerful.

I have come to believe that we all have our unique rhythm in life. Often others have tried to teach us to dance to their rhythm rather than ours. This can cause us to be out of sync. In my experience, when someone is out of sync too long, they become exhausted with life. When I find myself soul-exhausted or heading down that path, I ask myself, "Where is my rhythm?" Soul-exhaustion has taught me to become self-aware and to accept myself. For me, I spent life as a people pleaser, afraid to be abandoned. Can you imagine how easy it was for me to dance to the rhythm of other people? Often, I didn't even realize I was doing it. This became so deeply ingrained in my life that I would put up with so much pain to not lose someone. I didn't want to be alone and unloved. In the end, I was exhausted and encaged by my fears and longings. I was holding on too tight.

Over a year ago, my 17-year marriage came to an end with quite a painful blow to the heart. I knew deep down that it was done, but I wasn't ready to let go. I was holding on so tight. I wasn't sure I could manage the loss of all that I knew. It did end, and my life as I knew it was over. Much to my surprise, I made it. I survived what I thought I couldn't. My greatest fear realized, and I was okay. Was I okay every day? Not at all, there is a lot of grief in loss, especially painful loss. This loss was the great equalizer in my life. It was through this time that I was willing to look at the truth. I realized that I am an excellent storyteller. In an effort to protect my heart, I crafted a story about what was happening in my marriage. My story was one of hope and recovery for the sake of family. I held on to this story, unwilling to look at the truth right in front of me. When I was confronted with my ability to create protective illusions, I had to look deeper.

A deeper look is scary, it feels overwhelming and uncertain, but for me, there was freedom on the other side. Once I was able to accept the truth about why my marriage was ending, I was ready for the next layer of truth. How was I going to choose to respond? I want to say that it is purely out of the goodness of my heart that I have handled everything the way I have. The truth is that I was able to realize that I have a deep capacity for revenge, and I also have a deep capacity for love. I chose love. I choose to love my son more than I seek to inflict pain on anyone else. The freedom in this is that I am honest with myself to know that I am capable of both. I am capable of hurting others as much as they hurt me. For me, courage is to know what I am capable of and choosing the way of love, flow, and freedom. There is something so freeing to me to look at my potential for darkness and choosing my light; instead, it's the power of choice.

It was in this time and space that I was also willing to realize that my desire to belong and please people caused me to live an inauthentic life. The life I was living, my choices, and the beliefs I was practicing all came from other people and not me. This truth rocked my world. The time has come for me to be okay enough with myself that others can choose me or not, and I'm okay. Becoming the real me, that is where my deeper courage comes from, it's not an easy path. All of the ways that I am reclaiming my rhythm refresh my soul.

It feels a lot like my life ended last year, and the sting of that can still be raw, but a new day is here, a day in which I get to choose to be fully me. I get to choose to be in my flow. I am still learning the sound of my rhythm. Now and then I get off track, but I am learning to listen and feel my way home to myself. I hope you will allow yourself to be okay no matter where you find yourself today.

Chapter

Eighteen

Tales of the Mysterial Heart
By Maria McGonigal

Maria McGonigal

Maria McGonigal was born in Portugal during a fascist regime and became a daughter of the revolution. She was born Maria da Piedade, which translates into Mary of Mercy. Maria has an insatiable desire to bring beauty into the world. That is her sustenance. She has sailed the seven seas and has made pilgrimages to various ancient power spots in the world. After meeting the love of her life, Rian McGonigal, she moved to America.

Maria has been crafting a variety of transformational offerings, created to catapult people into living authentic and graceful lives. Maria is a teacher of inter-connectedness, providing others with missing pieces, energetic or physical, connecting them with their soul so that they can find their answers. She focuses on bringing different, yet integrated systems together to create harmony, balance, and healing.

Maria is praised for her keen intuition and profound wisdom. Her teaching style is direct, dissecting, not suitable for the faint of heart, yet full of heart. Be ready for long-lasting transformation, which demands a willingness to acknowledge what has been lurking in the shadow and holding you back.

Maria's deepest desire is to create a safe, sacred space to discover the most glorious and magnificent version of yourself. She offers unique training, retreats, workshops, concert meditations, and personal sessions in Prescott, Arizona, and power spots around the globe.

Maria lives in mystical Prescott, Arizona, with her husband, Rian. They were married in majestic Sedona, Arizona, in 1996. They have recently adopted a mini poodle, Ziggy, who constantly reminds them about the power of unconditional love.

Maria McGonigal is a Soul Coaching® Master Practitioner and Advanced Trainer, certified advanced yoga teacher, and sound healing practitioner and trainer. You can reach Maria at www.mariamcgonigal.com.

Tales of the Mysterial Heart
By Maria McGonigal

Some crossroads change our lives forever. Without a road map, all we can do is listen and follow our courageous hearts.

It was New Year's Eve of 1993. Brilliant fireworks danced on the dark ocean, like stars in a windy sky. I was celebrating on the deck of the luxurious cruise ship, Crystal Harmony, anchored in beautiful Acapulco Bay. I was being transported into a dream state by the gentle waves and the magical bursts of color in the sky.

Destiny brought me to work on the Crystal Harmony cruise ship. My soul longed for the sea. I was born in Portugal and grew up fascinated by the stories of the Portuguese sailors' indomitable spirit and soul. Like the ancient, mystical explorers, we followed the sun. Without maps to follow, they followed the stars.

Their adventures led them into new worlds across the oceans and within themselves. I found myself navigating the same waters of the heart. The privilege of living on the sea was a treasure I will forever carry in my heart.

Nothing can compare to being lullabied to sleep by calm seas, or brought to your knees when storms reveal the rage of the ocean's unconquerable waters.

As I contemplated this adventurous life aboard the ship, it felt like I was entering a fairy tale of my imaginative childhood. I had somehow taken hold of a magic wand and manifested the desire to travel to exotic and mysterious places only found in my dreams.

The auspiciousness of this unprecedented New Year's celebration began stirring deep within me. I was beginning to feel restless.

I said spontaneously, "I don't know how, but this year, my life is going to change." This commanding decree departed my lips but was born in my soul. Ripples of intention stirred the waters of my womb. Nine months later, they bore fruit.

On September 13th of 1993, I met Rian. He came on board with his mother. The 13-day Mediterranean cruise was a birthday gift from her, and a get well celebration after his second bout with cancer.

When I met Rian, a fire ignited that could not be extinguished. His essence was like a melody played by a serpent charmer. I followed, enchanted.

We met where we could. We played ping pong on the ship, met at a romantic square in Portofino, Italy, mimicked the Titanic famous scene on the front of the ship (despite potentially being fired for bringing a guest to a prohibited area), and had divinely appointed encounters in empty churches in Sardinia.

On the last night of the cruise, we kissed goodbye in Venice. Rian promised he would write to me at every port of call, which he did. After my return to Portugal, Rian came to spend time with me and meet my family. He left with my promise that I would come to visit him in America.

But the day I was meant to get my Visa, I couldn't get out of bed without feeling completely dizzy. What was happening?

What paralyzed me? Why did I get sick right before my trip to Lisbon to get the Visa?

I was scared, confused, and disappointed. So, I went to our family doctor. After a lot of tests, he concluded I was fine. He asked me directly: "What is happening in your life? Anything unusual going on?" "Yes," I retorted with anxious realization. "I met a man that I am supposed to visit in America, and I think I am scared of what can happen." Kindly, he answered me: "Just go and visit your friend. If things don't work out, you can always come back to Portugal." I left his office with a smile and a spark of lightness in my feet. I said to myself, "Maria, go and see if this is only a lark or a real story. If it is a real story, make it a beautiful one."

Despite my resolution, fears arose: Were we going to get along? Was I going to move to the USA? How would I make a living? These and a million other alarming questions assaulted my mind, but nothing could stop me now!

My courageous heart was whispering, and I was ready to step into the void. I needed to break ties with my family, friends, and the land where I had spent the first 30 years of my life. My identity was dissolving.

Life is not about knowing all the answers or having the perfect plan in place. Living authentically happens when we fearlessly follow the whispers from our courageous hearts and take the next step into the unknown.

I moved across an ocean of sorrows and doubts, leaving my previous life behind to be 24/7 with someone I hardly knew.

We called our home the Crystal because of its many facets, and within this Crystal, we were to meet all the facets of each other's souls. Some brought us joy, delight, and the innocent love that comes with new beginnings. Others brought us to our knees with the intensity of unconscious and uncared for wounds that we didn't want to meet and were never meant to carry. But we promised to hold hearts, even when we couldn't look into each other's eyes.

We knew that our sublime love would demand and command us to rejoice in the rainbow colors and endure all shadows of a storm. Choosing not to have children, we were willingly facing, transmuting, and ending a long and painful karmic lineage.

On the other hand, our professional lives were full and filled with excitement. Rian was the director of the music and sound therapy program at the internationally-famous O. Carl Simonton Center. After being ostracized by the current medical establishment, Dr. Simonton established the first mind-body cancer center. Patients had the opportunity to discover and eventually accept numerous aspects of their personalities. Some behaviors were potential allies with cancer that manifested in the body.

I captured on video the seemingly miraculous, spontaneous transformations of the cancer patients, induced by the sounds activated by Rian.

Rian fell in love with classical guitar as a boy. He had mastered many classical pieces, played with orchestras, accompanied masterful singers, and won both rock band and classical guitar contests in high school. Rian brought experience and refinement of music and applied it to the emerging field of sound healing. He was now adding ancient sound sources such as the didgeridoo, drums, crystal and Himalayan bowls, and the voice. He worked with an extremely sick, cancer-patient population. Led by their courageous hearts, they came from all over the world. The allopathic medical community gave no hope to many. They came to work on their emotions and faced issues they had refused to accept. Many were facing their final life decisions. They were scarred from chemotherapy, radiation, and the devastation that manifests in the physical, mental, emotional, and spiritual levels.

For many, their energy was weak, as was the light in their eyes. I got to witness, time and time again, a fast and complete transformation in the cancer patients after only a couple of hours of Rian's sound healing magic.

Without a job, the most practical thing for me was to begin assisting Rian with his sound healing work. Our young egos were strong, and we forged into new territory. Our intuition and knowledge of how to communicate silently fully awakened.

We began creating fields within fields of sound and provided sessions to voyage through sound, exploring consciousness, relaxation, and healing. It was fascinating to explore our relationship as lovers, friends, sound healers, and business partners. A true labor of love that allowed us to integrate pearls of wisdom never before experienced. My heart was exalted and craved expansion to accommodate the accelerated growth. We wanted to add movement to the sound healing sessions to engage the clients from a passive to participatory experience. Yoga was the answer.

I began practicing yoga and loved it. After seven years of practice, a new member who came to try yoga approached me at the end of the class and asked me if I was a yoga teacher. Surprised, and almost embarrassed, I quickly answered, "Oh, no. Not me." She said: "You are truly good! You should be a yoga teacher." I had such deep respect for the yoga tradition and didn't see myself fitting the profile of an honorable yoga teacher. I told Rian about it, but quickly dismissed it and went back to my regular yoga practice. Not much time went by until I had a similar experience. Another new member came to try yoga, and at the end of the class, asked me if I was a yoga teacher. I said no, but this time my heart was pounding. I went home and told Rian, who promptly said, "Well Maria, you love yoga, you are good at it, and this is the second time this happened. Are you going to wait for the third time, or are you going to do something about it?"

Our vision to integrate yoga and sound was revolutionary and futuristic. I chose to train at the oldest yoga school in America, International Sivananda Yoga Vedanta Centre, still steeped in the ancient traditions to balance my approach to yoga. It was a one-month intensive training in California. We had been living together 24/7, and this was our first time apart in seven years.

I returned home exhilarated but apprehensive since I had no experience teaching. All I had was seven years of personal practice and a contagious passion for yoga, which opened a lot of doors. My first position teaching was at our cities' only yoga studio at that time. I went on to add health clubs, churches, and private homes.

Despite having no college degrees, I used the energy of my courageous heart to apply at our local college. I was accepted as an exception to the policy requiring a college degree. The first semester, I taught in Bagdad, AZ, a mining town an hour and a half away from Prescott, where I live. Undoubtedly a baptism by fire, my passion, and enthusiasm to share Yoga dismissed any practicalities. For over a decade, I taught thousands of students of all ages and walks of life.

Teaching for the college allowed me to create assignments and integrate my passion for art. The "Yoga Creative Projects" were born. The students had complete freedom to create a poem, dance, sculpture, painting, anything that expressed their experience with Yoga during the semester.

My forthcoming book, *Sermons on the Mat*, is the result of one of these fantastic projects. It is a selection of threads from notes that a student had written down over four years while meditating, breathing, and getting herself through hundreds of sun salutations.

The beginning of my teaching replicated one of my teachers. Slowly but surely, I found my voice and unique expression of the yogic teachings. In the book's introduction, I speak of these changes: "As the years progressed, my classes became less about a series of poses and more about honoring the moment and sharing life as it came. It became more about integrating the idea of a human being as an elegant, unified field of awareness comprised of much more than only the physical body. It created the space for that to be explored in a regular class. The poses were an inspirational springboard to wild discoveries into the mystery of the human body, mind, emotions, and heart."

This new approach to yoga yielded new experiences and results. Deep transformations began occurring in people's lives. After the class, students would be waiting, seeking further guidance, which I was eager to provide.

Excitedly, I shared the experience with my wise friend Pat who advised me, "The Universe is always striving for balance. When you give, you need to receive. It's a law. Otherwise, you are creating an imbalance in the Universe. Maria, if people ask for and trust your guidance, either call yourself an intuitive coach or get certified."

For two years, I researched life coaching certifications, but nothing resonated. One day, Soul Coaching® came up, and my search was over. Never in my wildest dreams would I think that my yoga journey would bring me here, to my next crossroad.

It couldn't be more perfect that the next Soul Coaching® training fell right during our summer break. Being on the right path doesn't mean our lives are not going to be challenged. The 2008 economic recession was now hitting the college. Our finances were compromised, and I needed to find a way to come up with the tuition for the training.

My parents are the epitome of generosity and have always helped family members and neighbors in need. They had generously supported me financially throughout my school days. I had let them know that it was now time for me to make it by myself, but they offered to help. I needed to swallow my pride and accept their help.

Being so far away in Portugal, helping to support me financially was one thing that brought them joy. It warmed their hearts to share their love in that way. I had taken that gift away from them. With profound gratitude, I packed my bags and went to California to become certified as a Soul Coaching® Practitioner.

When I returned to Prescott, I immediately began teaching the Official 28-Day Soul Coaching® program to my yoga students. Their transformations were astounding. By guiding my students to listen to their souls, this program helped them resolve issues that a yoga class could not address.

In the meantime, my teacher, Denise Linn, decided it was time to pass along the Soul Coaching® legacy. She created an Advanced training that is also a gateway to becoming a Soul Coaching® Trainer. I knew that I wanted to be one of them. My dear friend Pat, the instigator that propelled me in the direction of becoming a coach, had crossed the rainbow bridge. Unbeknownst to us, she generously included us in her will. In her honor, I used her gift to pay for my advanced training.

Two years later, I became certified as a Soul Coaching® Trainer, and I have been offering unique training since 2018. During these unprecedented times for humanity, there is a need for an everyday experience of spirit and a connection to the inner states of intuition, mystery, and wonder. This can bring forth new solutions to ensure the survival of our species. Soul Coaching® not only offers that connection but informs us that all the answers we need are already within.

I have always followed my heart, and have trusted my intuition, but when I found myself at a crossroad, I had beautiful people who came forth to nudge me in the right direction. Likewise, sound healing, yoga & Soul Coaching® guide and assist us in listening to our courageous hearts.

Chapter *Nineteen*

Conquering Fear Disguised As Self-Sabotage

By Iulia Mihai

Iulia Mihai

Iulia Mihai, MSc., CHt., is an internationally-respected coach, clinical hypnotherapist, and author. She is the founder of Success Path Coaching & Hypnotherapy in Vancouver, Canada. Iulia has over two decades of experience in the area of human psychology and behavior. She has held various human resources leadership roles with large corporations in Europe and Canada, and she now offers coaching, hypnotherapy, and meditation programs for personal growth and healing. Her passion is helping women get out of their way and stop sabotaging themselves to create a life and career they love. Iulia has lived in several countries and has worked with people of different backgrounds. They all had one thing in common: a desire to change their lives for the better by clearing their blocks and limiting beliefs to experience personal transformation and achieve breakthroughs. Check out more of Iulia's written work in the best-selling book, *The Grateful Soul: The Art And Practice Of Gratitude* (available on Amazon).

If you wish to connect with Iulia or want to share your experience with self-sabotage, you can reach her via:

Email: iulia.coach@gmail.com
Website: www.successpath.ca
Facebook: https://www.facebook.com/successpathnow/

Acknowledgments

I would like to express my gratitude to Jane, my wonderful mentor, who passed away many years ago. My life would have taken a completely different path had I not met her when I did. I carry her memory in my heart, and I am forever thankful for her guidance, support, and unfaltering belief in me. I know she still watches over me. I also want to express my thanks and gratitude to the many teachers and mentors who have inspired me over the years: Deepak Chopra, Sandra Ingerman, Jeanie Martin, Martha Beck, and so many others whose gifts changed me forever.

Conquering Fear Disguised As Self-Sabotage By Iulia Mihai

Courage is a lot of things. It is taking a leap of faith and going after what you want, even if you don't know what the outcome will be. It is trusting your intuition, your gut feeling, your heart even when your head says otherwise. It is doing the right thing, no matter what. It is believing in yourself and knowing you are enough even when someone tells you otherwise.

Just as courage is many things, so is fear. Have you ever set a goal to eat healthier or start a new workout regime or stop smoking, only to quit a couple of weeks later? Or perhaps you decided to work on an important goal like finding a more fulfilling job, or starting a business, only to talk yourself out of it a month later? Convinced yourself that you're not good enough, or that it's too hard or not the right time to reach that goal you've always wanted?

If any of this sounds familiar, you, my dear, have fallen victim to self-sabotage. Which, to be clear, happens to the best of us.

So what exactly is self-sabotage, and how can you break the cycle? Self-sabotage is one of the many faces of fear. It keeps you from fulfilling your dreams and goals, and it tends to show up when you lack confidence, have low self-esteem, or you're afraid of failure or rejection.

Self-sabotage shows up as the excuses we make for why we didn't do something. Those excuses present themselves in our behaviors and actions. We say we want one thing but do the opposite because, on a subconscious level, we don't truly want it to happen.

In a sense, it's a battle between our conscious mind (wants and desires you're aware of) and subconscious mind (thoughts, emotions, and beliefs running in the background). It's a frustrating cycle, and it happens to all of us, regardless of our good intentions.

The good news is you have the power to stop self-sabotage and show up in a way that will help you lead a more fulfilling and happier life.

Here are five things you can do to stop self-sabotage:

1. Commit To Change

We all know change is hard and that it's easier to stay in your comfort zone than to try something new. But, if you truly want to change your life, setting clear and specific goals and sticking with them, especially when things get uncomfortable, is a must. As Jim Rohn said, "Motivation is what gets you started. Commitment is what keeps you going." From my experience, I know this to be true: if you're *committed* to making a change, you'll find a way. If you only *want* to make a change, you'll find excuses.

To manage your big goals, which will require sustained long-term commitment, break each of them into small manageable chunks (or "turtle steps"), and commit to completing each of those smaller chunks in a specific timeframe. Aim for frequent micro wins to keep you engaged and excited. Be realistic and don't overcommit because overcommitting always leads to overwhelm, which is the fast track to giving up on your goals.

Aim for progress, not perfection, and keep moving forward—one foot in front of the other. You will make it.

2. Hold Yourself Accountable

The best and easiest way to hold yourself accountable is to ask someone else to be your accountability partner. This can be anyone you trust who is willing to support you: a friend, a colleague, a business partner, or a personal coach.

Communicate your turtle steps and timelines to your accountability partner and ask them to check in with you regularly to see if you're doing all the things you committed to do. Most importantly, ask them to give you tough love when you need it. Because you will, trust me!

I won't sugar coat it, things may start easy and seem exciting at the beginning, but soon enough, you'll hit a snag, and suddenly you'll think, "It's not as easy as I thought it would be." It's in those exact moments that you will grow and expand and become a better version of yourself.

You don't evolve when everything comes easy; you do it when the going gets tough. When you are in challenging circumstances, the best and most resilient version of you is being born. Look back at your life, and you will see that the tough experiences you went through were probably some of the most transformative moments in your life.

So keep pushing forward, even if you need a few days to regroup, and remind yourself why your goal is important to you, why you're doing this. What is your why? Such an important question to keep asking yourself when you feel like giving up. When all is said and done, you will only fail in life by failing to try.

3. Remember Awareness Equals Power

Making excuses, complaining, blaming others, and procrastinating are all ways you're sabotaging yourself. Pay attention to negative thoughts and behaviors right when they happen and notice what triggers them. Is it possible to avoid these triggers completely? Or can you find a way to quickly get back on track after a trigger temporarily derails you? What is the antidote to your triggers?

Being aware of what causes you to self-sabotage is the first step towards minimizing or eliminating a negative or limiting thought pattern or behavior that no longer serves you. The truth is that your limiting beliefs serve a purpose, and that is to protect you against failure or rejection. Noticing your negative thought patterns and starting to question their validity can bring not only awareness but also the strength to keep moving forward.

Awareness always equals power. Let this become your mantra going forward.

4. Surround Yourself With The Right Support System

What if you've tried everything and still can't seem to stop getting in your way? Then take a look at who is around you. Often times, people who succeed have access to the right support system, whether it's a mastermind group, a mentor, a coach, or someone they look up to who inspires and encourages them to push themselves outside their comfort zone.

As a hypnotherapist and coach, I know shifting your mindset is easier said than done. It's easy to get derailed and give up—continue doing what you've always done. But that is not going to get you where you need to go. Remember, what you're not changing, you're accepting.

If you have tried everything, but there is still a limiting belief that rears its ugly head when you least expect it, consider working with a hypnotherapist to help you uncover when and how that limiting belief came into being, and how you can eliminate it for good, both on a conscious and subconscious level, so you can get out of your way, stop sabotaging yourself, and get crystal clear about the strengths you have.

Wanting to do better or telling yourself to do better is not enough. Sometimes you need to update your unconscious mind programming that is running in the background so that it is aligned with what you're trying to achieve. Then you'll be able to propel yourself forward into the life you've only ever dreamed of.

Coaching both the conscious and subconscious mind is hugely important because, ultimately, 95 percent of your behaviors are pre-determined by your unconscious programing.

5. Let Imagination Be One Of Your Superpowers

Einstein said that "imagination is more important than knowledge." I would add that it is also more powerful than logic or experience. Everything you'll ever create in your life will first start in your imagination.

Your thoughts create your circumstances, not the other way around. If you tell yourself, "I can do it," you can. If you tell yourself, "I can't do it," you can't. They are both equally true.

Change your thoughts and shift your mindset, and your life will change too. Let imagination be one of your superpowers and allow it to expand the way you see yourself, think, and behave, so that your life is enriched and transformed beyond what you thought possible. When you transform your thoughts, they transform your feelings, and together, they transform your life.

One of my favorite shamanic teachers, Sandra Ingerman, once said that one way to handle negative and fear-filled thoughts about things that haven't even happened yet is to ask, "Is this thought coming from love, or is it coming from fear? And is this causing me to separate, or is this causing me to feel more connection?" Connection is what humanity is all about. When we allow our minds to go into fear, we disconnect ourselves from everyone else. This makes us feel like we are all alone, and we have to figure it all out by ourselves because no one else is there to help. That is fear talking. If you feel that way, come out of your head and back into your body. Touch your chest and feel the beat of your heart, take a few deep breaths and focus on the here and now. If you can, talk to a friend or someone who is supportive of you. Come back to this moment now, instead of allowing yourself to spiral into the future that hasn't happened or to relive the past.

I know dealing with negative thoughts is difficult for many of us. I've experienced it myself, and I have seen many of my clients struggle with this as well. That is why I would like to leave you with one technique that will help you challenge your negative thoughts so that you're able to release them, and get the emotional distance you need from any painful thought. It is remarkably easy to use, but it works surprisingly well. Let's get started.

1. What is your painful thought? What is the thought going through your mind causing you distress? Try to summarize it in one brief sentence.

For example, let's say your thought is, "She doesn't care what I think."

2. Say this thought out loud and notice how it feels in your body. Notice what emotions come up when you believe this thought.

For example, if you say, "She doesn't care what I think," you feel angry, sad, disheartened. Your chest feels heavy, and your breathing becomes shallow.

3. Now, replay your thought with this phrase in front of it: "I'm having the thought that—" Repeat all of it a few times out loud if you can. You can also do it in silence, in your mind, if you are surrounded by people and unable to say it out loud. I find that saying it out loud and hearing it is more powerful than saying it in your mind.

Our example becomes "I'm having the thought that she doesn't care what I think." Repeat it a few times.

4. Now replay your thought one more time, but this time add the phrase, "I notice I'm having the thought that—" Repeat all of this a few times and let it sink in.

Our example becomes "I notice I'm having the thought that she doesn't care what I think." Repeat it a few times.

What happened? Did you notice any sense of separation or distance when you replayed your thought with these phrases in front of it, "I'm having a thought" and "I notice I'm having a thought"?

I bet you did. It's amazing how becoming the observer of your thoughts pulls you out and helps create emotional distance from the painful thoughts you are having. Practice this with other painful thoughts, and notice how you are able to distance yourself from the story you are telling yourself, and perhaps even release those thoughts. Recognizing that this is your story will give your mind the opportunity to be the observer rather than react to the painful thought.

I would love to hear from you. What triggers—people, situations, and thoughts—cause you to self-sabotage out of fear of failure or rejection? Are you allowing yourself to show up 100 percent, not knowing what the final outcome will be? Or are you living small to avoid failure and potential heartbreak? Because the truth is that living small will eventually make you feel like you failed and that, my friend, will cause you heartbreak. So you might as well live large, be bold, be fearless.

As Dr. Brene Brown says, vulnerability is not weakness. On the contrary, it is the best measure of courage. Imagine what your life would look like if you woke up every day ready to show up, despite feeling vulnerable—no excuses, no complaining, no holding back. Imagine what that would feel like in your heart and in your body. How exciting that would be!

Well, today is the day! As you're reading this book and hearing all the wonderful stories about courage in its many forms, remember that you have the ability to act from a place of power and choice, not from a place of non-power, which is fear-based—the choices you make every day matter. You matter. Starting today, commit to living the life you want, and say no to self-sabotage, one small step at a time. You can do this!

Chapter *Twenty*

My Courageous Heart Journey

By Maggie Morris

Maggie Morris

Maggie is an authentic caring, sensitive soul with a passion for nurturing others with her soul love. Maggie lives her gifts of service to humanity through her generosity and her ability to ignite the flame in others to see their limitless possibilities. Maggie uses her intuition and connection with spirit to be an example of strength and courage to all she meets. As an author, public speaker, life coach, mindfulness mentor, meditation facilitator, and death doula, Maggie continues to pursue her passions, as well as helping those she connects with to find healing. You can reach Maggie through her website at www.whispersofwisdom.ca.

Acknowledgments

Special thanks to my good friend Anne Joannette-White for challenging and inspiring me to write a submission to *The Courageous Heart*. I am deeply grateful for her encouragement, along with her belief in my abilities, even when I lack belief in my abilities. She is a courageous life supporter, for which I extend much love and gratitude.

I want to always acknowledge my creator, angels, spirit guides, and ancestors for guidance throughout my life. The words I write come from the meditations of my heart and soul. I am always grateful that they continually show up for me.

I add a special acknowledgment to my family for their love and patience with me for all those times in life when I did not get it right. I am thankful that our family is a circle of strength and love, learning that every crisis faced together makes the circle stronger, not weaker. I love you!

I'm thankful for the tribe of people in my life who celebrate with me as I endeavor to passionately live my authentic life: a tribe who accepts me as I am, faults and all.

Lastly, I am so totally grateful for the wonderful opportunity to work with Todd and Kyra Schaefer at As You Wish Publishing. Their love and support inspire all writers, not only some writers.

My Courageous Heart Journey
By Maggie Morris

As I sat for many days contemplating what to write for this book, my mind was flooded with memories of the times in my life that I was called to summon that courageous heart. Having a courageous heart is a choice we all must make. I recounted a few times in my life when I was faced with that choice in my book, *Journey to Soul*. I invite you to read that book, as I will try to not duplicate it here.

As I was writing that book, I was faced with a medical challenge that required a decision to have a courageous heart in dealing with my heart condition. I've known of this condition since the birth of my first child in 1987 when I found out I had a minor heart valve leak. I was told at that time I may have, in fact, had it since birth, though it was not detected until then. What a fantastic time to find out that you have an issue with your heart as you lay on an operating table about to give birth to your first baby! Sure, there was no added stress in that moment—you think? For many years, my life went on as normal except for the occasional heart echo to measure the leakage. That is, until this year, 2020, when all that changed.

After a minor infection had landed me at the hospital the previous year (which I had recovered from quickly), unknown to me, the cardiologist had ordered a follow-up test for the following year. When the call came for that test, I was sure that some mistake had been made, as I had not been to the doctor or been sick in that whole year. I was feeling physically and emotionally better than I had for many years. I had written my first book and was leading a meditation group. This was the best time of my life, and I was living my most passionate life. I have heard that most times, that's how illness comes to us, out of the blue, without warning, or even checking to see if you are ready for it. Let me tell you, I was not prepared for what was to come. Or was I?

To appease my doctor, I went for the test. Suddenly my world turned upside down and inside out. I was being told that in the past year, while living the absolute best year of my life, this leak had gone from minor to severe, now requiring heart surgery. Was this for real or a bizarre nightmare that I might soon wake up from? How was this possible? Other than a few dizzy spells, which I had assumed were blood sugar spikes, I felt wonderful. My head started spinning with all the unknown possibilities and outcomes. Being told that doctors did this surgery on a daily basis in no way made me feel any better. I did not want this surgery even if they were extremely skilled at it. The idea of my chest being opened, and my heart placed on a table for repair, was in no way within my life plan. Monkey mind had certainly made its presence known in my head. I was knocked off-kilter completely.

I shared this information with only a few people as I went inward to bring my body, soul, and mind into balance. I knew I could not stay in the place of panic where I now found myself. If there were ever a time to have a courageous heart, it was now. I had a choice to make, as often in life, we are faced with life-changing choices. Do I choose fear, or do I choose courage? Those seemed like the only two options in this “heart” dilemma.

As in many other times in my life, this choice was mine and only mine to make. It took a little while to step away from fear and self-pity, but deep in my soul I knew that the courageous heart was calling me to step up and live what I believed. As it had in the past, my courageous heart was calling me to be brave. It was reminding me that fear was not my friend.

All of us have had times in our life when we have succumbed to fear. All of us have had times when we allowed panic to take over. All of us have had times when we felt beaten down, in a pit of despair so low we could not see the way out. The fault is not in finding ourselves there; that’s part of human life. True despair is when we choose to stay there. Getting up from there while finding the courageous heart within yourself is your true sign of strength.

In my time of solace, the realization came to me that, although I could not control the situation that I was in with my heart condition, I certainly could control how I responded to it. That became my way of escape, the light that would lead me out of this state of fear and panic. That light would guide me to finding peace with whatever came. I decided that I would accept this challenge and learn all I could from it. Surely if this was brought to me at this most enlightened time of my life, it had a purpose. I would love to write here that this problem has been resolved, but it has not. I’m still living that journey and learning the lessons that it brings to me.

Choosing to thrive in whatever circumstance you find yourself is part of living with a courageous heart. I believe that those who have never faced difficult life challenges don't truly know if they have a courageous heart or not. Why? Because you never know if you have faith until your faith is tested or put through the fire.

To all of you reading my words—those who may be going through the fires of life at the moment—I implore you to embrace that courageous heart. Allow it to teach you and grow you into the powerful beacon of light this world needs. Become the person you need at this moment in your life! Is that an easy road? Hell no! But I guarantee it is the road that will give you the greatest return on your investment.

At every crossroads in life, we have the opportunity to choose the path we travel. Do we choose the easy path or the courageous path? That is the question. The courageous route may be lonely at times, as it might be the road less traveled. Both paths may lead us to the same destination, but be assured, in the end, the courageous route brings the most growth.

The courageous heart is a forgiving heart. Forgiving itself and others. How can we forgive others if we don't first learn to forgive ourselves? Forgive yourself for past mistakes, forgive yourself for what you did not know, and, above all else, forgive yourself for those times that you were not courageous.

The courageous heart is a loving heart. Jesus taught us that "love is patient and love is kind." Buddha teaches, "You, yourself, as much as anyone in the entire universe, deserves your love and affection." I read once that "we accept the love we think we deserve." Courageous hearts learn to love themselves, thus allowing them to love others in a deeper capacity.

Once we fully love and accept ourselves, imperfections and all, we are then capable of truly showing love to others. Until that point, our love for others simply mirrors the love we show ourselves. So, if you want to love others, I challenge you to courageously love yourself.

In my life, I learned that when I began to truly love the human soul that I was, my love for others began to flow from that. I became more patient, more understanding, more compassionate, more forgiving. I began to value others through the depths of my courageous heart.

Life can be a challenging jigsaw puzzle with roads often difficult to navigate, but the courageous heart chooses love over fear. The courageous heart chooses love over hate. The courageous heart chooses kindness. The courageous heart chooses patience.

The courageous heart is an encouraging heart. It lifts people up. Most people have no difficulty at all reminding themselves about all they are *not*, and as an encouraging heart, we can remind them of who they are. Encouraging others and lifting others up is what I am passionate about. The world becomes a better place when people believe in themselves. When someone believes in their power, they empower others. Life is not a competition; it's a community. We are all called to serve and raise each other up. The world works in harmony when we have a compassionate heart for others.

The courageous heart is a giving heart with a heart of compassion. Our world is a better place when we remember that we are neither higher nor lower than others, we are equal to one another. Often times, social status, money, and education lead people to believe that they are better than another, but I challenge that belief with my compassionate heart. Who we are at our core level isn't based on what we have; it's based on how we treat each other. One can have that courageous heart, whether rich or poor, as that courage comes from love.

Some may wonder, how do I find my courageous heart? Do I have a courageous heart? My belief is that every human born into this world has a courageous heart. It is in your soul. It is the breath of your entire existence, part of your DNA.

I believe that for some of us, our courageous heart may have been hidden by deep personal wounds. For others, it may have never been nourished and allowed to blossom into all that it was meant to be. For some, limiting beliefs have stifled its life, causing it to wither and appear dead. I believe that with proper nourishment (mindfulness, meditation, prayer, positivity, and personal growth), the courageous heart can sprout new roots growing into a powerful tree of life offering love, hope, peace, kindness, and faith to everyone it touches. I believe that at any age, a courageous heart has the ability to spark new life to those who may have lost hope.

How do we nourish that courageous heart, you ask? We feed it love. We feed it compassion. We feed it understanding. We feed it forgiveness. We allow our soul to grow larger than our ego. We give more than we take. We allow our soul to guide us to wisdom, and we allow that wisdom through experiences (often difficult experiences) to teach us how to love ourselves. When we truly love ourselves, our ability to love others grows naturally. Loving ourselves comes with accepting ourselves, faults and all. Forgiving ourselves for what we are not, gives us the freedom to become all that we are.

I believe life is a process; the same as having a courageous heart is a process. Does life become fundamentally easier merely because we have faith and a courageous heart? I wish I could say it does, but it doesn't. I can promise you, though, that faith keeps the light on. You may be surrounded by deep darkness now, but faith keeps that little flicker of light on, and your courageous heart grows that little flicker of light into a glowing ball of fire. A ball of fire that will ignite hope in you to lead you out of that darkness, forever changed.

I encourage you to ask your creator, God, spirits, guides, angels, and ancestors to continue to guide you on your journey of life. I challenge you to set the intention to ignite the fire in your soul. Set your course, buckle up, and watch where the Universe takes you. The journey of the courageous heart may not always be the smoothest ride, but it will take you to many amazing destinations.

When you set the intention to step outside your comfort zone, your courageous heart will lead you to new experiences. New adventures that you never dreamed possible will come your way. Who knows, you may even write a little book about your experience that will inspire others to find their authentic life (a little advertisement inserted to plug my book, *Journey to Soul*). But seriously, the only thing that limits you in this world is yourself and your limiting beliefs. When you let go of the "what if I fail" mindset, you have the opportunity to step into anything that your courageous heart desires. Yes, you absolutely might fail, but what if you don't? Failure is a good thing, not a negative one. We should be teaching that failures mean you stepped up and tried. It is more important to think "what if I succeed" and actually end up inspiring others to try new experiences by letting go of limiting beliefs that hold them back as well.

I challenge you to dream again. Dream bigger than ever before. Take chances. Follow the calling of your courageous heart and soul. As I said earlier, be that beacon of light you needed at the most desperate wounded time in your life. You can be the inspiring change that this world needs. Be the light in the darkness of your soul. Be the light of hope to others. Remember, the possibilities are endless. Be the ripple.

One who inspires courage in others is a valuable treasure in a world lacking hope. Your hope can be a lifeline to others who have lost the ability to dream. You can be the vessel to ignite their dimmed light. Your spark can touch their courageous heart, breathing new hope into it. That new hope will encourage them to also be the light, and the ripple continues to flow.

I have a picture hanging in my home that reads: "The soul always knows what to do to heal itself. The challenge is to silence the mind." Take time to silence your mind through prayer, meditation, music, nature, or whatever works for you. As you sit with that silence, your soul will speak. It will give you direction. It will give you wisdom. All the wisdom you need is within your soul, planted there by your creator. Seek wisdom, and you will find it.

Always mindfully remember that the courageous heart is a choice, your choice, and only yours to make. Circumstances happen, the journey you choose will always impact your life, as well as the lives of others. Every day, every decision is a choice we make.

I look forward to hearing from you as you make that choice to embrace your courageous heart.

Namaste

Chapter

Twenty-One

Your Soul Home

By Nicole Newsom-James

Nicole Newsom-James

Nicole was always a shy child and was given the CB radio handle of Bookworm by her adoptive father. Her grandmother gifted her with her first book, *The Arabian Nights*—a story of ancient mysticism revealing a lost treasure soon to become a theme in Nicole's life.

At eight years old, Nicole watched an episode of Star Trek entitled *The Empath*. The story was about an alien empathic healer named Gem, who saved the life of Dr. McCoy using her natural healing gift. Nicole was so impressed with the empath's healing abilities and self-sacrifice that she desired to be like her. Gem seemed like a superhero. Since Nicole believed in truth and justice and in helping those who needed help, she decided in that moment she wanted to be an empath too.

But first, Nicole had to experience life. After she entered the corporate world of oil and gas, she married and divorced in her 20s. She worked in the legal field in her 30s, before being spiritually called into the healing ministry in 1998. Nicole continued her spiritual healing studies by adding certifications in SRT, Chios, LomiLomi, and aromatherapy. She has also studied the 18 levels of Reiki and worked with the Sisters of Charity for over ten years at the RUAH spiritual retreat center in Houston, Texas.

Nicole was inspired to establish a spiritual retreat and healing center called Spirit Sense. For six years, Spirit Sense was a place for people to gather and learn alternative healing therapies for the mind and body.

Currently, Nicole is a co-author of four books, holds her real estate license, teaches online healing and space clearing classes, and lives in Oklahoma with her wife and three fur babies. She may be reached at 918-443-0592 or at www.YourSoulHome.com.

Your Soul Home
By Nicole Newsom-James

As small children, our stories end with, "and they lived happily ever after." As we grow older, we believe that life should reflect those stories from our childhood. If you are anything like me, you may have recently asked yourself, "So what happened? Where is my happily ever after?"

Well, believe it or not, the space we occupy, our home and work, has an enormous influence over our lives. In this chapter, I am going to give you some guidelines for creating a supportive soul space within your environment that will bring harmony, peace, and passion back into your life.

Everyone can intuitively pinpoint what is out of balance in their home or workspace. You might say, "No, you're wrong. I have no ability in this." I would reply, "Yes, you can, but something has blocked your ability to do so."

If you choose to join me on this journey, I will teach you how you can unblock your intuition and work through issues surrounding your home. The ensuing transformation will not only affect you but those you live and work with, including your guests. All you have to do is open your heart to move through the fear of change and allow your courage to guide you. Now let's begin.

Have you ever thought that taking care of yourself is how you can be there for others?

To be available and stay healthy through this process, you must establish self-care as a priority. One important part of self-care is the space in which you live. Your home should not be a place that you want to escape from; it should be a retreat that you want to escape to.

Does your home support you? Are you living the life you desire? Does your home support what you wish to create, or do you lose your energy?

Unwanted energies attach themselves to our homes, and we have lived with those energies for so long that we believe they belong to us. These unwanted energies can take on a life of their own, and since they attach to our life force, they may disrupt our energy.

What this means is that you may get ill, depressed, or you may feel anxiety and distress because of the energies. These energies may also affect your partner, children, or even your pets. Did you know that these unwanted energies may even keep you from selling your home?

What is a spiritual house cleansing?

I recently asked a past client whose home I cleansed, "What do you think of when you think of a spiritual house cleansing?" She said, "Getting out all the old and bringing in the gentle new." That sounds like a New Year's resolution, doesn't it? What she will now remember in her house cleansing was that her old energy and ideas, including past residents' residual energies in the home, were removed during the cleanse.

Once you remove old energies, then new energies may come in to support and empower those who live there. Whether you realize it or not, we leave our energetic thought forms behind in a home, including those from the previous people who lived there. Energies of arguments or depression can be harmful and what we call stagnant energy.

During a spiritual house cleansing, you remove the old energy. Once removed, the homeowner may intend to bring in positive energy for prosperity, love, joy, health, a new job opportunity, love interest, new goals, or directions in life, among other things. New energies then flow through the home and attract more positive energies.

Even before I obtained my real estate license, real estate agents called me to cleanse the energy of the homes they were selling because I am an energy shifter. Many of the homes, even though they are clean, repaired, or in good neighborhoods, wouldn't sell. So, I would do a remote spiritual cleansing on them. I would lift the unwanted stagnant energies, and then reset the home's energy to attract a buyer. Those homes always sold.

I asked one of my clients, Isabel Lopez, who is a broker in Houston, Texas, "Why do you seek to have the homes you are selling cleansed?" She said, "Just like we clean the house to have it ready for showings, I believe the environment and occupants have energy. I believe the cleansing helps to neutralize the energy and helps to tune in and set the intentions and the energy for a successful sale."

Isabel not only cleanses the homes she wishes to sell, but her home as well. She believes that when she spiritually cleanses her personal home, it helps her to find flaws and set the energy to support her, her family, and her business.

As an energy shifter, I have cleansed many environments, properties, and people. I can do this for you too. But in this chapter, I want you to take a spiritual journey through your home, within your soul, and with the tools, questions, and prayers that I have prepared for you to do your spiritual house cleansing.

Think about your life as a bunch of puzzle pieces. As you age, the picture changes. Some of the pieces do not fit who you are now. But you continue to hold on to those pieces as if they still represent who you are or who you thought you were. Think of it like this—the past has a certain picture and draws certain energy. A picture of you in your twenties looks different than a picture of you in your forties. Why would you hold onto a picture of you in your twenties? There are many reasons, but mostly it is human nature to resist change. Sometimes change can feel like we are falling apart. Sometimes this feeling is painful, and we want to be put back together. But what if we aren't a puzzle?

What if the pieces we are so desperate to hold onto like people, dreams, ideas, and careers are falling apart for a reason? What if you are not going through a *breakdown*, but going through a *breakthrough*? A breakthrough may be growing pains, and you are shedding the people and things in your life that are holding you back. Let yourself break through the old and become that person your soul is yearning to be.

One of the ways to shake off these old pieces is by taking a walk through the visual history of your life. Your home is the visual history I refer to because it reflects your soul. It shows your past, dreams, places you have traveled in life, and around the globe. To get to know yourself, let's take a conscious labyrinth type walk through your home.

A labyrinth is an ancient tool of spiritual growth through focusing on the inner self as you walk its serpentine path. I would like you to take such a walk through your home. In this journey, I want you to focus on the items you have collected and displayed in your home.

When you walk the labyrinth of your home, concentrate on what you would like to accomplish on your journey. Some people say a prayer and focus on empowering the prayer for their journey. Some set an intention of what they would like to achieve by the time they come to the end of their spiritual walk. And some walk through the labyrinth and notice how they feel through the winding journey. I invite you to choose one of these three approaches and set an intension of what you would like to achieve in this spiritual walkthrough.

I offer you this prayer to help you with the journey:

> For the spirit of my soul.
>
> I connect with the universal life force of all that is good and holy.
>
> I ask for divine guidance as I walk through the life force of my home.

> Give me the discernment to allow that which needs to fall away to be released, and that which empowers me, to stay.
>
> Thank you for this service and for allowing blessings and miracles to unfold.

Start at the entranceway of your home. You will need a pad and pen. I find the act of writing stimulates this process. Then take a leisurely walk through your home, noting any item that attracts your attention. As you walk, ponder these questions: How do you feel as you enter each room? Make a note. What objects—furniture, plants, figurines, or others—call your attention? Make a note. Continue your walk and taking notes as you move forward from room to room until you come full circle and reach where you started.

Now I would like you to grab a refreshing beverage and find a lovely place to sit and absorb your feelings. As you shift your energy, you may find yourself dehydrated, drinking a cool beverage will give you the needed pick me up to move through this session. Once comfortable, look at your notes and start with the first item you wrote.

As an example of the next step in this process, let's say you had a pair of embroidered dragons in a luxurious golden bamboo frame that you inherited from your grandparents. You might have noted that a memory stimulated when you looked at them. You might have remembered a beautiful story told to you on how they were acquired. Or, you might think of these dragons as Buddhist Nagas, ancient protective spirits of your home. But let's say you remembered your grandparents fought over these beautiful dragons because your grandfather was jealous of the adventurer who gave your grandmother such a valuable gift. Then you notice that you and your partner are having similar issues of jealousy. Interesting. So, do you see that the energy accumulated by an inanimate object can influence your life because it is in your environment? Your items have more power than you give them credit. They can empower you like a spiritual guardian or cause discourse, and throw you off track, unsettling you and those who live with you.

My friend, Father Brendon, who was a Greek Orthodox priest, had his vespers dry-cleaned at the same place that Houston police officers took their uniforms. One day, the dry cleaners caught on fire and all the clothes burned beyond repair. My friend tried to make light of the situation and went up to the owner and said, "I guess this is not a good time for me to pick up my vespers."

The owner said, "You're not going to believe this, but your clothing is fine. It survived the fire. No damage whatsoever." It was beyond belief that this happened. When I asked my friend if it was a miracle, he said that his clothes had the energy of his environment. You see, he was constantly in church praying for his congregation and community. His clothes were there with him in that holy space. The energy of the place eventually encapsulated and protected his clothing. Whereas the police are often around discordant energies because of crimes and domestic violence, so their clothes did not have the same protection. I have often thought about this true story and how important it is for us to be taken care of and be in healthy, supportive environments.

Now I would like you to go through your written list the same way as I did with the dragon picture and write down your feelings (all of them) and the memories or history of each item to learn the energy you are receiving from them. Should no thoughts come, open your imagination, and have a conversation with the item. Ask what it is doing to support you in your life, or any other question that might come to your mind, then note the answer.

Once you understand what objects are empowering you and what objects are disempowering you, then you may make an informed choice on what to do with those objects. You may discard or place the disempowering objects in storage, or you may hire a professional to cleanse them.

But before hiring a professional, if you do not want to let go of an item, you may try smudging. Smudging is a Native American ritual used to connect to the spirit world and cleanse the environment of unwanted energies. What you will need is a sage stick, lighter, candle, and a bowl with sand or water to put out the smudge stick at the end of the cleansing.

To start smudging, you will first light the candle, place the sage over the flame until it catches fire, then blow out the flame leaving the ignited embers of smoke. To cleanse an item, blow smoke over the item you wish to cleanse. The smoke releases the negativity and resets each item to be with positive energy.

To reprogram an item with positivity, state what you would like that item to do or represent in your life. Going back to the dragon picture, I would like the story of a beautiful guardian entity protecting me from harsh unwanted energies.

To do this, I would say over the item, "Thank you for protecting me and those I love."

So now you have walked through your home, noticed the energies of the items that caught your attention, discerned if they were empowering or disempowering you, then discarded or cleansed each one. There you have it, a simple system for you to cleanse your items and your home.

Congratulations on having a courageous heart. In cleansing the energy of your home, you have reset your environment to support you in the life you desire.

If you would like to take this information to the next level and learn more about spiritual house cleansings, I invite you to check out my website at www.YourSoulHome.com.

Chapter

Twenty-Two

Stepping Into Your Authenticity and Loving It

By Lori Nielsen

Lori Nielsen

Lori Nielsen is an international best-selling author on Amazon, and is an empowerment adviser and energetic healer. She has a Bachelor's Degree in Psychology from UC, Irvine, and holds an advanced certification in Ho'oponopono. She assists individuals with reclaiming their personal power through an internal process of healing soul wounds and ancestral wounds. She intuitively guides and counsels individuals of all ages to help them discover and embrace their authentic selves. Her mission is to teach individuals how to live their lives from the inside out with unconditional self-love, releasing all self-imposed limitations. Her experience is that once one identifies and reclaims their soul power, their light, they acquire the ability to stand unwaveringly in their power during challenging circumstances. One must own their light before they can securely hold their light, and then all things are possible.

You can reach Lori at OwnYourLight.org, and also watch for her soon on YouTube at Own Your Light.

Stepping Into Your Authenticity and Loving It
By Lori Nielsen

There are almost eight billion people on planet Earth at the moment I'm writing this. I'm looking at the Worldometer website and marveling at the rapidly changing "real-time" numbers worldwide, as births continue to tick up quickly, deaths tick up not as quickly, and the outcome of this simple equation shows the overall population continuing to grow steadily without pause. It's mesmerizing for me to watch. It's difficult to fathom how many babies are entering this world in this moment while I watch the numbers rapidly increase. Each baby, soul, is completely individualized and customized. Not a single human is exactly alike. Who are they going to be, and will they honor their differences?

When we are babies, we are completely authentic. We want what we want, and we freely express whatever we're feeling, usually with boisterous wails until our needs are met. Our survival depends upon it. As we develop, praise and punishment are the basic tools utilized to teach us the difference between right and wrong, which molds later behaviors that our families deem acceptable versus unacceptable, which can vary hugely. Personalities also respond differently to the input, and somewhere down the line, acceptable versus unacceptable often morphs in our minds into lovable versus unlovable. We quickly learn that if what we do or say is not accepted by our loved ones or peers, suddenly embarrassment or even shame can set in. A sudden loss of self-confidence and even self-acceptance is possible. This is the process of chipping away at who we genuinely are that occurs between birth and adulthood.

Beautifully individualized, confident, loving souls are born into bodies that are also equipped with egos. We are the only species on the planet with ego. It forces us to think before we act, which is necessary, but it is also the creator of fear and self-doubt. We overthink. We worry. We wonder if we are doing or saying the right things to be liked and accepted by others. We appear to be living in ego override, feeling uncertain, unfulfilled, or even unloved. The fear of not being enough is widespread.

I've observed this behavior in school-age children, and more specifically, mine. My heart sank the day my daughter decided to start wearing only black pants and simple muted colored T-shirts because she didn't want to be noticed, in other words, somehow stand out and be potentially judged or teased by her peers. My daughter is a funny, creative, and colorful person, an expressive artist. It was clear her fear of being unaccepted was beginning to overshadow her true sense of self. Suddenly what other kids thought of her had become more important to her than expressing who she truly was. She wanted to make herself small. I know this is common, but why? I started paying closer attention to the world around me and even began dissecting my responses and behaviors to the outside world. From children to adults, I observed at some level, *everywhere*, the fear of authenticity.

We fear we are not good enough. We fear we don't matter. A part of us wants to be seen, heard, and loved, but we are too afraid to show our true selves in fear of rejection. So we either remain small or behave in ways that we feel are most likable to others in search of validation. We look for likes on Facebook, we even change our appearances with injections, plastic surgery, body shapers, and photo apps. We pay for advice from "love gurus" who tell us how to act or what exact words to say to "get the guy." We slap on our make-up, squeeze into our Spanx, then hope for the best when the guy with the Porsche who can't pay his rent shows up for a date. What is going on? Ultimately, we want to be loved, and we are looking for it in all the wrong places for all the wrong reasons, and especially in all the wrong ways! Looking for love outside of yourself to fill the void inside, the one that is loaded with fear that you don't matter, or are somehow not enough, is an empty toxic loop. Also, like attracts like, so one empty human is attracting another empty human, and they wonder why the relationship doesn't work. You cannot give from an empty cup.

The saddest part about this is that as long as people are searching for validation outside of themselves, they will never be happy. They continue to make external adjustments and are focused on outside sources to fulfill themselves, which is an inside job. However, taking a hard look inside yourself is not always pleasant. There are wounds that require healing, and seeing yourself for who you truly are requires an open mind, a forgiving heart, and a degree of courage. We are all far from perfect.

You must be willing to look within yourself and sift through the emotional clutter to remove what is creating blockages to happiness and no longer serving you. It takes a level of courage to face your demons. If you never learned to look inside yourself, truly assess who you are, love and accept yourself, you have likely been busy living an external life attempting to please others in some form, fearful of judgment, and searching for love and acceptance. When things have spiraled out of control externally, it takes that much more courage to look internally. You likely will be faced with aspects of yourself you don't like and were avoiding all along because that felt easier. It's important to release the fear of what you might see or feel. Breathe. Be kind to yourself and trust the process.

You need to have compassion for yourself. Remember, you came here to make mistakes for the sake of learning and growing. There is no perfect person. Also, be patient with yourself. Moving from a space of conditioned fear to unconditional self-love is not an overnight task. It took time to wire your current thought processes. It will take time to unwire them and rewire new ones. Remember, this is your process, so move at your pace. Examine your past behaviors and reactions to others. What patterns do you see? What painful memories have continued to creep up all these years, and what memories have you kept pushed down and hidden because they made you feel small, like you weren't enough, or you didn't matter? Approach yourself through the eyes of unconditional forgiveness and love. Envision yourself as a small child feeling the pain you've buried, standing in front of you, hurting. Would you ignore that child? You know that child deserves love. Imagine opening your arms and embracing him/her, filling them up with all the love you've ever wanted and always deserved. This is you.

Facing your past experiences, hurts, mistakes, and flaws is not always easy, but if you approach yourself without any judgment, you will learn so much more. Watch your life and memories like a movie. See it for what it is, and then let go, forgiving yourself and forgiving others, with the promise to only remember the lessons to apply going forward. If you're angry with someone in your past who hurt you, it's important to move through those feelings as well. Avoid blame. Understand that they are a product of their past pain and circumstances too, and they have made mistakes. See this person separate from yourself, also as a child, experiencing their difficulties and pain. They are merely human, too, and struggling. Forgive them. Release them. We pass our pain onto others, which is also why it is so important to release it now. The past pains must be released to move forward in a new and consciously healthy way.

I also highly recommend learning the art of being present. Most of our suffering comes from our minds. Fear and anxiety come from looking into the future, bombarding ourselves with all of the unknowns. Depression comes from dwelling in the past, focusing on regrets and lack. Both conditions are a state of mind, overthinking. When we become present, right here right now, in the moment, all else disappears. We only have this moment right now. Both the past and future do not exist. They are thoughts and memories. Other than a genuine fight or flight response to immediate danger, fear is created in the mind. Get quiet. Feel your body. Feel your heart space. Breathe. Meditate. Once you learn to become grounded in the here and now, centered in your core being, mental fear disappears altogether. Meditation does not need to be complicated. Simply getting quiet, noticing the sounds around you, or tuning in to music will do. The point is to stop all thought. If you catch yourself daydreaming or thinking, which is totally normal, gently bring yourself back to the sounds upon which to focus. Practice this regularly. Any time you begin to feel anxious or stuck in your head, stop, breathe, listen, and feel the present moment. Let the rest fall away, as it does not belong here.

The next step after the process of releasing and learning to become present is learning to love yourself. Learn to live from the inside out instead of the outside in. Learn to make decisions from your heart space with intention. Live a conscious life. Change your approach in life based on the information you've discovered about yourself, specifically the things you don't like about yourself. A shift in perspective will shift your choices and ultimately shift your life. What feels right for you? Stay strong in who you are! Become the person you trust and admire for their accountability and authenticity. It will be challenging at times. There will be triggers. There will be moments of the same old fears of rejection popping up, especially when confronted with people you care about.

My current mental struggle is "What if they think I'm weird?" Working in the etheric world of energy puts me high on the list of likely to be judged as odd by others who do not operate in this arena. Most people haven't known this about me because it's relatively new, and I've hidden it a bit. Now I don't care if people find out, unless, of course, that person matters to me. Then fear sets in. Fear of rejection shows up like I've never done the internal work. That's when I ask myself, "Who are you truly, and is there any shame in that?"

No! I actually feel good about myself! And I love myself enough to not be deceived into believing I should be anything different. I am who I am, and I come from a loving space. If a person I care about decides they don't like who I am, it's best they leave my life now. I am committed to being my authentic self, and if I change that in any way out of fear of what another individual might think of me, that is a betrayal of self! Back to square one!

You were born enough. You were born lovable. You do *not* have to prove this to anybody. You *are* love. Know it and feel it in your soul. The love you've been looking for has been inside of *you* this entire time. Why do we care so much about what other people think? Who makes these people (who, by the way, are also exhibiting the same insecure behaviors) the experts of what's lovable anyway? Why do we give them so much power? Because that is what we are doing, handing away our power!

We fear judgment by others. The truth is, no matter what we do or say, we will always be judged anyway. So why not be your authentic self? Because it hurts less if you're judged for being your inauthentic self? When we put our true authentic selves out there to be seen, the judgment is scarier because it's more personal. We are putting our true, raw selves out there to be seen, and that takes courage. When we hold ourselves accountable to be authentic, we are open, wide open, and that comes with feelings of vulnerability.

Here's the awesome part, though. Once you stand in your truth and authenticity, people who no longer resonate with you will fall out of your life. That can feel not so fabulous at first but trust the process. If they stayed, it would come with a level of toxicity because you are no longer in alignment with them. While people who no longer fit your life naturally fall off, they are almost magically replaced with people who do fit your life. Your point of attraction has changed, and new people on your same vibration will show up. The people who love you for the *real* you. Welcome to your tribe. Your *authentic* tribe!

Are you ready? Courage is taking one step, stepping into your power. Nothing else matters in that moment other than your authenticity and owning it. Stand in your truth, in who you truly are. The first step is often the hardest. Feelings of vulnerability bubble up. But when what emotionally felt like certain death does not occur, you will begin to trust the process with repetition. And each time you are faced with a challenging situation, you have already created a new internal storyboard of how things will transpire. This time it's honest and true to self, regardless of the outcome. You stay true to *you*. Rewards come with this. It's time to take your power back! Living an authentic life is the ultimate form of personal freedom and self-love.

Trust and have faith that things will fall into place when you take this step. The Universe has your back when you stay in a space of love and authenticity. You were made to be you, not somebody else. When you step into your authentic self, the world cracks open with brand new opportunities made specifically for you. Opportunities that were not previously offered, because they didn't resonate with who you were before. You weren't aligned with them yet. These new opportunities will resonate with who you are inside, your true self, and it will feel *amazing*. Welcome to your new life. The one that fits your soul perfectly. You are *finally* free!

My hope as I continue to watch the Worldometer tick upward rapidly with new births, is that each of these beautiful souls remains true to themselves. That their parents do the inside work on themselves so that they can assist their children to express freely, bold enough to be the unique individuals they were created to be, from a space of unconditional acceptance, forgiveness and love. No courage necessary. No fear. Simply breathe, take the step, and *be*.

Chapter

Twenty-Three

Saying Yes to Self by Moving Forward

By Elias Patras

Elias Patras

Elias is an author, empowerment coach, motivational speaker, psychic medium, and facilitator for the *EmPower You* retreat series. As the winner of the 2019 Celebrate Your Life events Speaker's Program, Elias had the honor of sharing the stage with Denise Linn, Sunny Dawn Johnston, Lisa Williams, Anita Moorjani, Dr. Joe Dispenza, Dr. Bruce Lipton and Matt Kahn at The Celebrate Your Life Sedona retreat, November of 2019.

He has been studying energy work for over twenty years, including completing an apprenticeship in Peruvian Shamanic Studies, as well as currently co-facilitating an Earth Honoring Altar apprenticeship program.

His commitment and passion for teaching content that promotes growth and exploration of self are unequaled. This work has a clear focus on how we co-create our life with the divine and deserve everything that we want for our highest good.

He is also the creator of a specialized line of energy balancing sprays, manifestation candles, and inspirational bath salts to enhance areas of the mind, body, and spirit in being balanced and aligned.

In his work as a psychic medium and intuitive, Elias believes the key to learning and personal growth is how to listen and to connect to the signs and signals that we receive. His mission is to help others understand and tap into their intuition and inner voice.

Website: www.EliasPatras.com
Email: Elias@EliasPatras.com.
Social media:
Facebook www.Facebook.com/EliasPatras/
Instagram @Elias_Patras.
Also, follow him on YouTube.

Saying Yes to Self by Moving Forward By Elias Patras

Take a moment to breathe. A good inhalation and exhalation. Excellent. Now breathe from your heart. Place your hand on your heart. What do you feel in this moment? Can you feel the warmth of your hand against your chest? Do you feel your heartbeat? Is it racing? Is your heartbeat a nice steady beat? Now, think of the love that you have for yourself. The love that nobody but you can give to yourself. How does that feel? Is this an uncomfortable or an unknown type of thought? What do you feel when you breathe from this honored, treasured place?

When working with my clients, I find that we forget about putting ourselves first because of the fear of being selfish and judged by others. When we are in a relationship, I find that it is so important to find the love of self first. A good idea is to come to an understanding, a knowing, that we deserve to put ourselves first, and to love ourselves more than enough to show up in our relationships wholeheartedly. I find that part of this is to let go of the fear of not being good enough, of not being perfect, the fear of failure, and the fear of being alone.

What I have found is that most of us learn that we must find that *perfect* relationship, have a *perfect* wedding, and live a *perfect* life. From what I have found, this sets us up for high expectations in a relationship. The truth is that relationships are work. They are two people coming together, sharing their ups and downs, their passions, their joys, and also the feelings that stretch from one end of the spectrum to the other. The work that is done is like a dance. In this dance, we learn how to move with one another and find that unique harmony and balance. We learn to create a rhythm with the dance of our hearts, both individually and as a couple. The problem happens when we are offbeat, or our beat isn't heard or acknowledged. It happens when we express our individual dance and want to make it fit the dance of our partners. What may occur for some is that we put our dance away and simply dance our partners' dance, and we, unfortunately, lose our beat. Some of us even see the potential in our partners, and then we knowingly or unknowingly say we are going to fix them, to have them become who we think they should be. We, then, are not sincerely honoring their dance for where they are in their life. The question then becomes, how can we fix them if they have ballet shoes on, and we are wanting them to learn tap. This is not solely found in marriages, but in all forms of relationships.

In my experience, I have found that when doing work on ourselves by breaking through the fears of failure, success, abandonment, loss, judgment—whatever it may be—there is that connection of accomplishment. We can feel that empowerment in our body, mind, heart, and soul. That wonderful part of us that we say *yes* to ourselves, and we say *thank you* to the Universe for supporting us on this path. We can feel so good that we can want or feel the need to take others on the journey with us. The intention is pure, the part of wanting to create a better relationship is there, but what if the other person's mind frame is not there. Do you wait? Do you offer suggestions?

Do you ask your person if they want to go on this journey with you? Or do you put them on the path and drag them along? Depending on how you were brought up, this could be something that is done. We all learn from what we have seen and heard. What we have to realize is that your person has a choice in what happens. Like the old saying, "You can lead a horse to water, but you can't make it drink."

I want to share a story about a person who is near and dear to my heart. It's a story about being courageous and saying yes to moving forward. I have known him all my life, and we are extremely close. There have been judgments, and possibly some bumps in the relationship, but when all is said and done, I honestly do love him with all my heart, bumps and all. I will take you through the stories of love and how each love builds on another as he moved forward. Going through all these experiences with him have been life-changing for me.

His story starts with a loving household. Even though he was an only child, he was not spoiled in a materialistic way, he was spoiled with love. His parents were such devoted parents, so good-natured, and so giving to others. He learned so much from them. Both parents were opposites, but the qualities that he had from both blended so well. It truly, to this day, makes him a well-balanced person. The love that was structured for him was well-rooted within. He learned some amazing traits, a few habits that needed work, but all and all, he came from a genuinely loving home.

We move forward to his twelve-year relationship. During that twelve-year relationship, he had the honor of being a step-parent, which was a true gift. What a joy to see him help out with two beautiful children. The challenges that came along with raising kids are the common ones, but a true gift to witness, nevertheless. Within that time of this relationship, he lost both of his parents. One parent passed away. The morning of his mother's wake, the nursing home told him that his father was being rushed to the hospital too, and then, 15 months later, his other parent dies.

These two people were his rocks, his foundation, and where he received love like no other. There was a deep sense of loss within him. A loss that was heavy and that made the days drag on and on as time went by. Late at night, he said, was the most difficult time because all was quiet in the house, and he could hear the many thoughts in his head. All of the should haves, could haves, and would haves came rolling across in his mind. Several years passed after his parents' deaths, and that relationship ended.

Seeing him going through the transition of loss once again was difficult to witness. This did allow for some great conversations over the phone and some deep soul searching was acquired during that time. He was now alone. He had to move through the grief process that continued with his parents and his relationship, and start to connect to the strength that his parents instilled in him. So, he continued working on self-healing and started facilitating additional workshops based on his experiences and teachings. There is an old saying from an indigenous tribe in Chile, the Mapuches. They say that your healing is my healing. He truly felt this with every class, workshop, or retreat that he facilitated.

He dated here and there, and finally found someone else who was into bettering themselves and participated in many self-help seminars. I remember how excited he was to find someone who shared a lot of the same principals as he did. I can remember how he was intrigued about finding out more about these seminars.

Three months later, he went to his first seminar. This seminar taught him about trust, forgiveness, setting personal goals, how to be accountable, and asking for support when needed. I remember how impressed and how focused he was after this four-day seminar. The other retreats that he went on were more spiritual and emotionally-based in nature. These seminars, from his perspective, were on the emotional and intellectual mindset. I feel that the work that he did in the past and combining it with the seminar allowed for the two of them to get closer in their relationship as a couple. The seminar went so well that he decided to go do the next seminar, which was a full week seminar that would go even deeper than the first one. When he came back from that week, he started to find his voice. He realized that he was guilty of people-pleasing and putting himself last all the time. He didn't want to rock the boat in any way, so he would be the yes person. Looking back, I can see how pushing down his voice made him doubt himself and seek approval from others.

I don't know if that realization of knowing that no is a complete answer was enough for him to realize that he was in a controlling relationship. How things had to be done a certain way or they were not right. It truly hit him when he was given the choice of going to his best friend's fiftieth birthday celebration or his partner's mother's seventy-fifth birthday, which was on the same day. He felt that his friend would understand, and he should go to the seventy-fifth birthday party. He wanted to do both, but was told that was not an option. From that day forward, he started to speak up more. He had the courage to say that his opinion mattered, and there needed to be compromise in the relationship. That lasted for about five months, and the relationship ended.

The courage to be able to speak up and be heard was the second block that was removed from the wall of loving self.

As time passed, he was feeling the need to find the one, the special one to be with forever. After being on several dating apps and going on many coffee dates, he found someone that he genuinely clicked with. They laughed, and they mixed well with one another, but there was something a bit odd, but he couldn't put his finger on it. So what's a fellow-Mediterranean to do, but fix the person that you're with. Show them all the love that you can so they know how fantastic they are. Make them feel appreciative so that they know how special they are to you. He offered to have a narcissist move into his home. Slowly that second block comes off of the floor and starts to get recemented quickly. The lesson was not fully learned, in my opinion. The Universe wanted him to move through this, so it offered a person that would truly challenge him and make sure that he learned this lesson. One the narcissist got what was needed, a new place to live at a lower cost, things changed in the relationship quickly. Within six months, the relationship became stale. I remember him saying, this is not what I want. I need the narcissist to leave and get out of my life. The next day he went to have a talk about how the relationship is not going anywhere, and it was best if he lived by himself. The narcissist stood up, hovered over him, and said, when are you moving out?

I remember him sharing this story and saying, "When am *I* going to move out? I have lived here for seven years; you need to leave." The narcissist even had the nerve to call the landlord and say I would love to stay here, and I pay my share of the rent, I should have a right to stay here. The landlord said, "It's his apartment, the lease is between him and me, not you. You have thirty days to vacate, if that is what he wants from you."

Moving day came, and when all the narcissist's things were out of the apartment, something truly groundbreaking happened, he reclaimed his power of his place. He told several of his friends that he took frankincense and blessed each room. He called back the peace and the calm that each room had for him. He vowed that he would never give away his power again. A friend then said, "Didn't the narcissist take it from you?" and he said, "No, I gave it away freely just to feel a special kind of love, but it was never there."

I now take you to the most recent relationship of my dearest and wonderful friend. This one started off like all the rest, but there was an intensity that happened in the beginning. Not only was there a connection on an emotional level, but also spiritually. All of his friends said, "What a beautiful couple you are together; you complement one another." Things were so wonderful for him for the first year. As time went on, he noticed that there was something not lining up in this relationship. Small things at first. He found his voice from the last relationship and was able to present things in a communicative way. He took ownership of what was his and made suggestions on how to come to win-win situations. He even suggested that they do the personal development seminar together. This person said, "I will go, and I feel that I can do this on my own." Came back and said, "That was so good, I am going to go to the next one." Came back from that and said, "Here's what I want to tell you, and sorry, I kept these things from you." There was ownership, there was open communication that lasted for a few months. They got married, and things seemed to be in alignment again.

A few weeks passed, and something from the past was brought into the light. My friend was so deeply hurt. He wanted to know why did that happen, why was there a shift in the relationship? Words were said, and my friend realized he has to find the courage to leave this relationship. I was shocked when those words came out of his mouth. How could he leave this marriage? Where would he go? He would be alone again. Could he survive? I recall him saying, "It's because I love myself more than enough that I have to leave this marriage." He had to have the courage to move forward. He knew that nobody was going to complete him. He was already built that way. He said yes to himself and truly felt it. No shame, guilt, or confusion this time. Moving forward into the security of self-love by following the beat of our heart. He found the love in him that was given to him by his parents and healed the should-haves in his life by moving forward.

Chapter

Twenty-Four

The Courage of Forgiveness and Grace

By Dr. Carra S. Sergeant, LPC-S

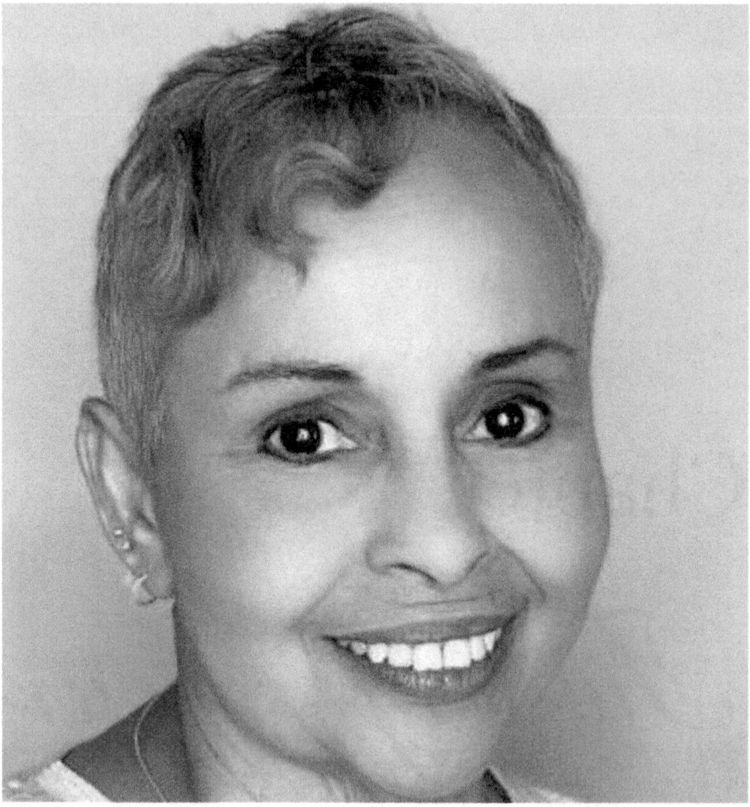

Dr. Carra S. Sergeant, LPC-S

Carra Sergeant is a "when life gives you lemons, add vodka, and make a limoncello" kind of woman. She is daring, caring, bold, and, at 67 years, people may call her old. Carra lives in Louisiana with her life partner, five dogs, three parrots, and two cats. She enjoys boxing, quilting, and reading. Carra's alter-ego, Dr. Carra S. Sergeant, is a Licensed Professional Counselor, a Certified Clinical Hypnotherapist, and an Access Bars Practitioner. She is the owner of Peace from Pieces Counseling Center, located in Lake Charles, Louisiana. Dr. Sergeant works with teens, adults, and couples, and is particularly passionate about facilitating healing from trauma and helping clients work through anxiety disorders. You can reach out to her at peacefrmpieces@gmail.com. Details on all services provided by Dr. Sergeant can be found at

www.peacefrompieces.net.

Acknowledgments

Thank you, Nannelle Noland, for your unwavering love and support over the last 24 years. To my parents, James and Susan Sergeant, both deceased, yet still extremely present in my life, I love you. My brother, Glenn Sergeant, is my rock and is the greatest brother in the world. I have no words to express my deep love for you. Thanks to my nieces and nephew, Monica, Ashley, and Glenn, Jr. To Jerry and Kacey Noland, I am so proud to be your M-2 and the alternate g-mom to Kassidy and Braden. My other mom, MeMe McKerley, is a special blessing in my life, as are my extended McKerley family members. My special star sister, Sandra Castille, has been my best friend for more than 30 years and has an indomitable spirit that has buoyed me through many rough moments. Lastly, I send a special thank you and buckets of love to my super spirit sisters: Karen Woodard, Andrea Vidrine, and Sarah Brink.

The Courage of Forgiveness and Grace
By Dr. Carra S. Sergeant, LPC-S

I was blessed to have grown up in a home where "unconditional love" was expressed daily. I learned that giving unconditional love presupposed the ability to grant forgiveness and offer grace when offended, hurt, or harmed. I felt like I had mastered this notion as a young adult. When I met someone, I accepted and loved them "as is." If they hurt my feelings, I could easily offer forgiveness, because I believed the slight was probably unintentional. I also learned early on that life was hard and left us all damaged in one way or another. This belief allowed me to offer grace because, in my mind, only hurt people *hurt* people, and that we were all hurt in some way. I granted this allowance to anyone I allowed into my life because, at its core, this was the true meaning of unconditional love. This deeply held belief allowed me to live a mostly happy and inspired life. I truly loved the notion of wearing "rose-colored glasses" throughout my life!

I sometimes questioned what would happen if someone entered my life, thru no choice of my own, and inflicted inexcusable harm upon me. Would I still be able to offer the same unconditional love? Would I be capable of offering forgiveness and grace? If I could, would that make me a saint? If I could not, would that make me a fraud? As life would have it, I would one day be presented with a situation where that choice had to be made.

Forgiveness is the ability to consciously release feelings of anger, hate, resentment, or vengeance towards someone who has harmed you. It does not require anything like an apology or admittance of wrongdoing from the other person. Forgiveness may not have any real value to the transgressor. Forgiveness is an internal choice, a deliberate decision that sets you free from a prison of hate, rage, and powerlessness. Forgiveness is the first step in regaining your command over the event and the effects of the transgression. Forgiveness does not erase the incident but allows you to look at it through softer eyes, and in that way, it provides a powerful liberation.

Many people perceive forgiveness as a sign of weakness, in that it sets you up for repeated hurt by the same person. However, forgiving someone does not mean that you forget or excuse them for their wrongdoing. It means that you have chosen to set boundaries to lessen the probability of a repeat offense. Even victims of lifelong abuse can benefit from granting forgiveness to their offender. However, healing without forgiveness is indeed possible. Forgiveness is a choice, not a prerequisite. The value in allowing forgiveness to occur is that, in releasing the negativity, you no longer let an event or person to color inside the lines of your life. It gives you the freedom to create a life unburdened with long-term pain, rage, fear, and bitterness. Forgiveness is all about you. It allows you to open a space in your heart that you can fill with love, joy, peace, and compassion. It enables you to break the chains of victimhood and live an unfettered life.

Although I have been able to forgive those I love, forgiving the stranger who harmed me has proven to be a daunting task. It was an act of horrific brutality that changed me to my core. It awakened in me a virus of fear that, for a long while, inhabited every inch, every corner, and every cell of my being. I was easily startled by any sudden noise, fearful of being alone, yet equally afraid of being around anyone I did not know. I feared the dark, and I was scared to sleep because that stranger would haunt my dreams. Not a day went by where fear was not my primary underlying state of being. This single event almost changed everything I believed about the inherent good of all people. I pondered the existence of evil and wondered what I had done to deserve this brutality.

Carrying this toxic load of hate and humiliation and self-recrimination took its toll in every way imaginable. My mental health suffered as there was no "physician heal thyself" happening inside my head! As a therapist who understood the value of talking, I chose to remain silent. The fear of talking made it real, so I convinced myself that ignoring the pain would, in time, heal the hurt. Instead, it had the reverse effect. My soul became angry, and I mean viciously angry. Any imagined wrong would set me into what I called "scorched earth" mode and woe to anyone who found themselves in my direct line of fire. I lost my ability to temper my anger through the filter of loving kindness. My physical health suffered as my body slowly began throwing one health crisis after another at me. For five years, my mind screamed, and my body railed against me as it sought relief. I was unwilling to yield.

Then, one day, I woke up and found myself sick and tired of being sick and tired. The hot lava that had been bubbling in my core had reached critical mass and exploded into a volcanic primal scream. In that one torturous moment, I released the poison that had been trapped inside. I was now ready to tell my story. My reliable support system quickly rallied around me, and the seeds of forgiveness and grace that my parents had planted were released into a healthier environment in which to grow.

Everyone's forgiveness process is unique and personal, but we all take some similar steps while on the path to forgiveness:

- We realize that forgiveness is a choice, not a mandate. That it allows us to move forward in life with intent and deliberation;
- We understand that forgiveness and reconciliation are two different things: Forgiveness does not require us to allow a person in our vicinity. It is okay, however, to allow reconciliation to occur, if you choose to;
- We believe that everyone has some inherent value, even if they hurt us or hurt someone we love. In that mindset, forgiveness becomes an essential part of recognizing and respecting the humanity in everyone;
- We address our pain and acknowledge the harm that has been done. Facing our suffering head-on provides an opportunity to reframe its impact on our life;
- We find meaning in our suffering. What good came from it? For many of us, we become more resilient. I am not minimizing the damage; I mean that we can use that pain and turn it towards something good;

- We allow ourselves time. Forgiveness is a process, and depending on the depth of hurt, it can be a long one. We need to be gentle and patient with ourselves during this time;
- We stay focused on the fact that we reap the benefits of forgiveness, and do not give up;
- We remember that this choice to forgive will enable us to develop a mindful and forgiving heart.

So, where does grace enter this picture? Grace is also about letting go of past wrongs that we have endured. The act of offering grace, however, takes forgiveness one step further. In offering grace, we find the ability to offer well wishes to the person who caused us harm. Grace replaces the need for vengeance or retribution. Grace removes our innate need for "karmic retribution." It is an essential component of spiritual health and healing. It allows us to rise above the trauma so that we can pray for someone to receive the happiness we may not believe they deserve. Grace reawakens our hope and reignites our passion for love and life. To give grace to someone is to provide them with undeserved kindness and mercy, even if you feel they deserve hate and punishment.

Grace is also more than a reaction to an adverse event. Grace is a state of living. From a religious standpoint, grace is a level of divine forgiveness, conferred upon us by God, for the sins we have committed. From a broader universal perspective, grace is an exquisite state of being where we begin to realize that a divine energy higher than ourselves is present in our lives and in that moment.

When we are hurt, harmed, or injured, we want to exact retribution. As a spiritual being having a human experience, it is natural for us in that humanness, to be angry and hateful in the face of pain and fear. Grace keeps us from descending into a pit of acid that dissolves our soul. In moments when I have been able to offer grace, even to my aggressor, I have felt a fresh breeze of divine peace. The experience is so spiritual that I feel this peace move *through* me and *into* the other person.

Grace seems to be easier for me than forgiveness. You see, while grace and forgiveness are linked, they are also autonomous. One can occur without the other. I can look at the person(s) who caused me pain and see through their woundedness and offer them grace. Depending on the depth of pain, forgiveness then becomes a whole different process. But again, that is because offering grace provides peace.

Grace allows me to show up as my authentic self every day while still being aware that my authenticity allows me to be vulnerable. Offering grace does not make me superhuman or better than anyone else. It simply helps me create the kind of happy, peaceful magic that I want in my life. My choice to offer grace may seem selfish, and in one sense, it is. However, when I allow grace to flow through me, the other person receives a special kind of energy from me that says, "even though you have hurt me, I still honor your divine humanity." The offender is not necessarily consciously aware of that energetic message, but their soul will receive it—when it is ready. Until then, it sort of resides in their spiritual inbox.

Offering grace means offering love and light. It means that we choose not to react to our oppressor negatively. It means that we choose to overlook the knocks and the bruises. It means that we choose not to *give in* to the voice in our head that wants us to re-experience the pain over and over again. It means living a life with good intentions for and toward everyone. It means choosing to walk away sometimes, even when it is hard to do.

I am not perfect at this by any means. I am just like you, and therefore, as I honor your divine humanity, I must also honor my divine humanity. I have to offer grace to myself, and that is hard because it feels vain and self-serving. Yet, if we don't take care of ourselves, we can't take care of anyone else. Therefore, I do it because it is the healthiest way to take care of the divine energy that resides in my soul. If I don't honor myself, then I cannot truly honor you.

Offering grace helps us create a kind, caring countenance that directs us to live a life of love and compassion. If we allow grace to be the driving force of our life, our life becomes charmed and beautiful. We learn to live in the now, experience serenity, embrace the warm fuzzies, see the miracles, and bridge the gap between chaos and balance.

How does one live a life "in grace"?

- Realize that as humans, we are all wounded in some way. Seeing someone as a wounded being allows us to develop empathy for them.

- Find hope in our heart for all wounded beings to find our way towards healing.
- Make the hard choice not to "clap back," even when it is our natural inclination to do so.
- Remember that offering grace is a spiritual decision, not necessarily a religious one.
- Offering grace is offering our best self to others. Isn't that what we are called upon to do?
- Grace is offered unconditionally. There are no levels. You are either "all in," or you are out—no judgment, no shade.
- Open your eyes and look around you. Grace is everywhere if you can allow yourself to see it. Grace *is* us if we allow ourselves to be it.

Now that you have a brief snapshot of living a life of offering grace and processing pain into forgiveness, you can understand why these are easier choices when dealing with someone you love unconditionally. That still leaves the question I proposed early in this manuscript: "Would I be capable of offering forgiveness and grace to someone who entered my life and inflicted inexcusable harm upon me? If I could, would that make me a saint? If I could not, would that make me a fraud?"

Saint versus fraud is a hard choice, fraught with sharp edges. To choose either as the correct answer assumes that either or both decisions are made 100% of the time. It feels like forcing myself to choose is harshly unfair.

I assure you that I have never felt like a saint, but have often felt like a fraud. In processing the source of trauma that prompted me to write a chapter for this book, I can say that yes, I offered grace to the person who attacked me. Conversely, however, forgiveness was five years in the offing. Since unconditional love includes the self, I first had to offer grace and forgiveness to myself. I forgave myself for holding on to the pain for so long. I offered myself grace so I could reconnect to my divine energy. Whenever I speak to my clients about the value of forgiveness, I tell them and remind myself that sometimes, we end up being both saint and fraud.

As the memory of the pain faded into the background of my life, I convinced myself that I had forgiven him. Ah, the lies we tell ourselves. In the volcanic eruption on the day that my anger broke free, everything shifted back into perspective. In that precise moment, I realized that I had been so busy trying to forget the pain that I had hardly even begun the process of forgiveness. I took the first few steps quickly: I talked, I screamed, I allowed my spouse to hold me while I cried, I sought support, and I had my chakras rebalanced during a lengthy energy healing session.

I am still a work in progress, but I am ready now. That day of reckoning was Day One of a new life for me, for on that day, I started my adventure down the yellow brick road toward forgiveness. Traveling this path, I do so as the embodiment of both the Tin Man and the Cowardly Lion, for at the end of my journey, I will be rewarded with a genuinely courageous heart.

Chapter

Twenty-Five

The Diamond Inside

By Allison Voth

Allison Voth

Allison Voth is the founder and director of HoneyHeart Company, established in 2020. The creation of her company began with a clear vision to serve others on their healing journey through her streamlined services. Certified as a Transformational Grief Coach in the F.L.O.W method through Denise Dielwart's Academy. Allison brings her gentle guidance and natural gifts to Coach adults beyond grief after a parental loss. Additionally, she is certified as a HeartMath Personal Resilience Coach, and a 200hr RYT Yoga Alliance Teacher. All of her programs are designed for anybody willing to take the next step on their journey right now. Before becoming an Entrepreneur, Allison garnered over 20 years of experience in the Canadian federal government. Serving for 14 years as a civilian for the Royal Canadian Mounted Police, five years as a Volunteer Auxiliary Constable and, one year as a Border Services Officer. Her law enforcement background, combined with her parental loss and pain, evolved into a journey that uplifts, sustains, and supports our inter-connectedness both locally and globally. Her passion is cultivating heart-to-heart connections through nurturing our common unity of un-conditional love. Like honey, we bond our communities through our unique expressions. Leaving a legacy of love helping others to connect with joy is her greatest treasure. Allison resides in White Rock, British Columbia, Canada, and can be reached at www.honeyheart.ca. Her custom meditations are available exclusively through the Mindimension app. Details at www.mindimension.com.

The Diamond Inside
by Allison Voth

This is the story of my future, from the perspective of where I am right now, not from the narrative of where I have been. Unraveling the deep mystery of the heart's journey is one that can only be charted through the power of navigating the grand sea of mystery in the waters of the unknown.

Embarking on your healing journey requires a will to summon courage from the ineffable well of truth within you. You will not find it in spending your days liking and re-sharing memes on social media or talking about what others are talking about. It means, going to the most painful place to ask the deeper questions, to query your soul for the information you are so desperately in search of, but even with all the asking, you are still unable to find solace after spending countless hours wondering why you don't understand someone else's perception or actions. It was never about them; it is about you discovering what *you* are made of.

Compassion stems from the growth of discovery. Curiosity sets you free to explore a new map of reality. Through my experiences, I learned that our heart is a compass. Developing listening skills is to tap into your innate intuitive power, unmatched to any other guru. The word—heart—itself, broken down into an equation reveals: HEAR-T. Are you listening to your heart speak? If it could talk, what would it say? Invariably it will lead to your heart's true north to your truth. This is what I call the north star, and it is brighter than any diamond on earth. When we ask our soul instead of Google, we turn on our inherent magnetic power within to process our greater self. Nothing else, no one else has power over you. In so many ways, life imitates art. We are the artistic expression of the divine in infinite possible experiences. We come from pure love, but our conditioning covers up our greatest treasure, much like layers encasing a diamond.

Diamonds are created from extreme pressure and heat to crystallize. The challenges in life present you with two choices—love or fear. Everything stems from those two polarities. What you feel could cause you anxiety and stress, so it may be time to take a moment and touch your heart center. Breathe. Listen. Feel. Transformation can only begin in the heart when you are willing to touch it and feel what comes to the surface.

Through the process of going through the FLOW (Feel. Let go. Overcome. Become Whole Again) Transformational Grief Coaching Program, not only have I learned to coach others in this process, but I went through the most astounding deep experience I could have imagined. I could never have known that life would send me these profound lessons to learn, and more importantly, tests to overcome.

I registered for school in February, and the day my classes began, the pandemic was announced by the World Health Organization, and the world shut down. Learning to cope with the pandemic life in lockdown alone triggered deeper layers of fear and grief. As I adjusted with the contraction of the external environment, I observed the mirror of life within my internal environment. I battled all the thoughts associated with fear and anxiety, "I'll be single forever, "How will I create a new business?", "What is going to happen to my mom?" Having a senior mother with Alzheimer's living one hour away by herself is another challenge thrown into the mix. While we are cast into the unknown, the way to draw back to our pure heart center and learn is to begin with acknowledgment.

Do you know that big elephant in the room? Its name is fear. If you don't acknowledge it, it can spiral down into disease and disharmony with the natural flow of life. I could never have known I would be given the gift of being pressured, like the diamond, to a greater potential. I lost half the mental clutter weighing me down by tossing out old beliefs, thought patterns, negative behaviors, and material "things"—deep-cleaning my mind and physical home with removing all that was no longer serving the present. Going through the FLOW program was such a beautiful blessing to begin to lead me first before I could begin to reveal the light of expanded wisdom, I gleaned through processing and transforming those layers.

Adjusting to our new normal took me a few weeks while also beginning my new career without the cushion of a day job. The risk was great, but I had the courage to be all in! I believe in healing and helping others, so one day I simply acknowledged that elephant, I looked fear in its eyes and said to it: "I recognize you are there, thank you for being here to teach me." Then I had a hot bath and allowed feelings to flow. Often, this first step is what we spend our lifetime avoiding. Distracting ourselves with external muses or comforting ourselves in unhealthy habits. Within hours I felt an amazing shift within that was only possible through that first step of acknowledging fear's presence. The feeling begins the healing. Letting go is the next step.

Surrender is an incredibly powerful act of faith in God, source, the Universe. Whatever your doctrine is, you have wisdom you can access at your fingertips, literally. Touch your heart, breathe, feel, and acknowledge your teacher's presence. Your heart will guide you to let go and surrender to this greater consciousness. You have accepted the lesson, like a leaf laid down on a gentle stream, you let it go to begin overcoming the belief that you are separate from the well of pure love within you, your inner guru. It requires an expansion of understanding that life will only teach you when you are ready for the next lesson, bringing you closer to shining your beautiful heart light. Every effort is like taking out a polishing rag to get in the nooks and crannies with some elbow grease to ultimately see a sparkle.

Our heart becomes encrusted as rough stone, a diamond is not discovered as a sparkling gem upon unearthing. Before the cutting and polishing process, a thorough examination of the diamond is conducted. Like a dull piece of glass, we must work on polishing the edges to remove layer upon layer of stories, conditioning, pain, suffering, and identity to worldly views of who we think we are. Therefore, a process must take place to fulfill our greater awareness of truth and to "know thyself" and our purpose in this lifetime. Your ability to integrate comes from your courage to explore.

Are you curious about what is outside your comfort zone? I can tell you firsthand that there is joy, fun, playfulness, and lots of smiling on the outside of that zone. My absolute favorite energy to be in is creative playfulness. No fear exists within it, and I feel safe to bring new ideas to life and share them with others. To embody a light-hearted feeling is to become the true expression of your heart's desires. Pure love only has one desire, and it is to be expressed. Your diamond begins to shine magnetically and draw in more energy into your life. It's truly magical and humbling to experience and 100 percent worth the growing pains. Trust me, I have been there and got the t-shirt, and I have given them away. I am done collecting t-shirts!

Losing my dad to a sudden death on his 68th birthday in November 2015 brought me to a precipice of asking the big questions. What is the objective of life? Why are we here? What is my purpose? Eventually, I found myself where I no longer wanted to believe I was broken. I was searching for whom I knew I could be. The burden of understanding love is heavy; it is even heavier than the dense emotion of grief. You have to open your eyes to seek the truth, and only then will the answers slowly unfold. I struggled for years to overcome this choking emotion of grief, threatening every day to drown me. I thought when I lost my dad—my best friend—that I had lost my unconditional love connection. Sensitivity is a gift; I learned that the hard way after his death, along with my engagement being called off and saying goodbye to that partner. Now, in my forties, I have learned to become my own master after a long journey harnessing difficult emotions and transforming them into beautiful diamonds and pearls of wisdom.

One of my heirloom family gifts is the mermaid cross-stitch my late father made me in his life. He had unmatched patience to hand-stitch large works of art with beading. Imagine a beautiful large turquoise mermaid with pink and purple butterfly wings, sparkly green thread and pearls and jewels sewed on to her skin. As she comes up from her deep dive, within her hands, she is carrying her treasure of diamonds and pearls, but there is one that is greater than all. In the center of her hands is a heart jewel sewn on. She discovered that the greatest treasure of priceless measure is her heart.

When you reach this step in FLOW, you have already laid the groundwork, the neuropathway to your new life, embodying love because you begin to understand you are made of love itself. Those trillion cells in your body vibrate and feed on pure love alone, like sweet honey; otherwise, they are dying to be expressed. All they need is our love. The burden is the collective consciousness seeking a way out of disbelief in our power, we have to lead the way with our inner guru, trust our greatest treasure, and allow it to shine and show others the path. I believe in fostering relationships through our inter-connectedness and sharing our gifts to nurture the whole.

Together we weave the golden threads that create a net for others to surrender into pure love. Trust is the golden net we create by living our new way of life which fosters our symbiotic relationship within life—it catches us and teaches us to not let others fall through it. We strengthen it through connection. I serve with a passion for keeping the net golden, for lending a hand to others to step up and sparkle. Nature is always working towards homeostasis. Note "working towards." It takes the constant effort of life and us as individuals to act upon choices that serve the greater good of all. Gather a tiny grain of sand and imagine the cosmos in your hand. It only has the power if you believe in it, like our hearts.

The heart is our quantum processor to the greater mind. When we turn it on with our arrow of intention, it sends signals to the brain. Like sonar in dolphins, our brain sends signals out, and then pings off our brain when we receive the information as feedback. Feedback is then stored into our diamond heart to be wired into our operating system. I'd call that an upgrade, wouldn't you? Also referred to as the "a-ha moment," this is the exciting experience that information has now become integrated to cause a transformation. Your perception, actions, and expression will change as a result. It sounds like a fun adventure to me to keep exploring and asking if there is more love to give! Generating an expanded awareness provides the fertile ground to plant new ideas, create a vision, review your values. To express it and put your passion into action, you can create the energy that allows you to feel others' stories, to hold space for them by embodying compassion.

An important key that helped me recently was re-framing unconditional love into pure love. Words have power, and unconditional still implies conditions within the mind. To remove all focus and switch the perspective, I only refer to the highest form of love as pure love. When you ascend to full glory, your brilliance is your influence on yourself and others. All the angles and cuts of your diamond heart refract our unlimited potentials, waiting to be brought into form and into expression. To celebrate life is to acknowledge and accept the dark and the light within me as my inner guru. Between the polarities of black and white, lie every potential you can imagine. As life would have it, I gleaned that I am living in the polarity of having no goodbye with my father's sudden death, and navigating the longest goodbye while managing my mother with Alzheimer's disease. You may be thinking, which scenario is worse? In response, my heart speaks to you and says this one thing—neither of them. They are both teaching me how to find the courage within the infinite potentials of expressing pure love at any given moment, regardless of challenges.

Within my toolbox of self-care, my number one priority is to be in nature and meditate. My father instilled in me a deep appreciation for nature, we were always hiking, biking, and going for long walks. Somehow, we always ended up at Dairy Queen eating banana splits, but at least we burned some calories beforehand!

I live by the sea on the Pacific west coast, and I love watching the ocean change, the eagles circling in flight, tuning into the subtle sounds of hummingbirds, and stopping to smell flowers. Self-reflection is a natural part of my daily thought process; I am constantly reflecting throughout my day and able to catch myself falling through that golden net of trusting my heart. Feeling all that is important, and I acknowledge when I need to set boundaries for my self-care practices. Connection with my local community has also made room for creating a network of appreciation and gratitude on a deeper level. I find peace in making choices that sustain my community through purchasing local food, products, further reducing the need to go elsewhere for "stuff." I've developed a meditation group and have bonded with many business owners through simple acts of kindness.

My passion for helping others along their heart's journey evolved into me using my poetry as a form of expression to create guided meditations in collaboration with the Mindimension meditation app. I have several options you can choose from to relax into the golden net of trust, to have a silent reunion with your parent who has passed, and other heart-centered meditations. These range from five minutes for beginners to one hour for a deeper dive exploration.

Returning to our inherent state of wholeness, I ask to please remember this quote by Anais Nin: "Life shrinks and expands in proportion to one's courage." To truly embody pure love, is to evolve. Discover your journey to wholeness and joy with me, right now. You don't have to suffer through grief alone, learn to FLOW with me and discover your diamond heart.

Final Thoughts

It is a distinct honor to work with authors who are committed to making the world a better place. We at As You Wish Publishing adore the authors in this book and feel they make a difference every day.

Keep writing dear friends, your messages are needed now more than ever. Trust that what you have to say will be used to make a positive change for everyone you meet.

Thank you dear readers who have found the courage to allow the wisdom in these pages wash over you and soothe your troubled heart and mind. We are with you!

With love and appreciation,
Kyra and Todd Schaefer

Want to write your own book?
Check out our EZPublish Package at
www.asyouwishpublishing.com/ezpublish

Made in the USA
Middletown, DE
23 October 2020

21807031R00169